THE COLLECTOR'S
BOOK OF BOXES

OTHER BOOKS BY MARIAN KLAMKIN

Flower Arranging for Period Decoration
Flower Arrangements That Last

THE COLLECTOR'S BOOK OF BOXES

By Marian Klamkin

Illustrated with photographs by
CHARLES KLAMKIN

DAVID & CHARLES · NEWTON ABBOT

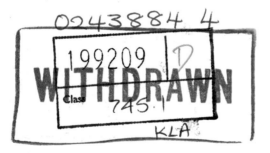
ISBN 0 7153 5420 5

First published in the United Kingdom by
David & Charles 1972

© Marian Klamkin 1970, 1972

Reproduced and printed in Great Britain by
Redwood Press Limited
Trowbridge & London

ACKNOWLEDGMENTS

Without the cooperation, aid and encouragement of many individuals who share my love for beautiful boxes this book would have been most difficult to write. To all those old friends and the many new ones who opened their homes and allowed their collections to be handled and photographed I am most grateful.

The staff of the Watertown (Connecticut) Library, particularly Mrs. Caroline Stark and Mrs. Marian Sumner; Professor Dan Calabrese of the Art Department of the University of Connecticut; and Mr. William H. Watkins, Director of the Mattatuck Historical Society, Waterbury, Connecticut, are also deserving of my appreciation and gratitude.

If this book is successful in being informative and entertaining for collectors it is due in large part to the efforts of my husband, Charles, who patiently photographed all of the boxes illustrated and was, throughout, supportive and encouraging.

I would like, also, to express my gratitude to two men whose efforts in behalf of this author deserve more than mere recognition—Mr. Allen Klots, Jr. and James Oliver Brown.

The boxes photographed are from the following collections:

Beatrice Alexander, 16 (bottom left), 98 (bottom left), 99

Author, 4, 5, 15, 17 (center), 19, 20, 24, 65, 72, 76, 79, 85 (bottom left), 91, 93 (top left), 98 (top left), 106, 111 (top left & right), 113 (bottom left), 114, 117 (top), 124, 127 (bottom left), 128 (bottom right)

Mr. and Mrs. Robert Belfit, 89, 90

Jo-Anne Blum, Inc., 102 (top), 104, 105

Mr. and Mrs. Richard N. Fried, 51 (bottom left)

Mr. and Mrs. Arthur Greenblatt, 11, 12, 13, 14, 17 (top left), 23 (top), 30, 77, 126 (bottom), 134 (bottom left & right), 136

Ellena Hall, opposite page 1, 2, 3, 17 (bottom), 29, 33, 39 (top), 44, 46 (top right), 51 (bottom right), 52 (bottom left & right), 53, 55 (center & bottom left), 56, 66, 69 (upper left), 102 (bottom), 106, 108, 120, 126 (bottom right), 129 (top right), 130, 131, 132, 138 (top right)

Marjorie Hardy, 86

Leo Kaplan, 7, 26, 28, 34, 35, 37, 41, 42, 45, 49, 50, 52 (top), 54, 55 (top left), 57, 58, 59, 70 (top), 71, 73, 78, 103, 123, 127 (bottom right), 128 (bottom left), 129 (top left)

Jean Ludeman, 121

Marie Whitney Antiques, 6, 63, 64, 70 (bottom left & right), 80, 85 (bottom right), 138 (top left)

Mattatuck Historical Society, 8, 21, 40 (bottom), 61, 74, 82, 83, 84, 87, 90, 93 (top right & bottom left and right), 94, 96, 97, 98 (center), 100, 107 (bottom), 111 (bottom left), 112, 117 (bottom), 118, 119, 126 (top)

Ludy Spero, 46 (top left), 69 (upper right), 107 (top)

Joanne Theiner, 43

Mr. and Mrs. James M. Troy, 18, 23 (bottom), 36, 39 (bottom), 135, 137

Jane Weber, 37 (upper left), 111 (bottom right), 113 (bottom right), 134 (top left)

CONTENTS

THE COLLECTOR'S
BOOK OF BOXES

(Above) *Swiss bird box, enameled silver. Although box is Louis XVI style it was made in 1900.* (Below) *Box is key-wound and when switch on front is tripped, top opens, bird pops up and sings.*

Chapter 1

INTRODUCTION

FROM the time when man first began to accumulate personal possessions he has required something in which to store them. From the need for a safe and easily transported container evolved the ubiquitous box. Boxes have been made and used for so long that it is not known when they were first made nor can the origins of the word "box" be traced. In ancient Egypt and Rome storage boxes and chests were made and artistically decorated for specific purposes. Between the eleventh and the eighteenth centuries Italian goldsmiths and jewelers designed and made magnificent boxes of precious metals and stones to contain the remains of saints and popes.

As civilized man began to wander, the box became extremely important as a means of taking his possessions with him. A portable enclosure for his belongings was a necessity. The box, a most simple piece of furniture having four sides, a bottom, and a hinged or removable lid, has never really been improved upon as a means of moving and storing goods. While the most primitive boxes and chests eventually developed into our many forms of case furniture, we still look for old and beautiful boxes to use as decorative accessories for our homes and for storing our own treasured possessions.

A study of boxes is a study of the changing values of civilized man, for by learning about the various uses of old boxes we acquire knowledge about those things that man felt were his most precious belongings. The Venetian merchant used velvet-covered coffers in which to keep his silks and other valuable goods from the Far East; the money-changer had an elaborate chest made in which he kept his gold; the vain eighteenth-century French or English dandy owned an

1

elaborately decorated gold box in which he kept the patches he used to hide his pox scars, and other boxes to hold his snuff or his perfume-soaked sponge. The Puritan came to America with his precious Bible enclosed in a specially made wooden box.

While the most common material for making boxes has been wood, there have been boxes made of just about any other imaginable material. Boxes of marble, porcelain, ivory, gold, silver, and semiprecious stones have been made. Often the value of the box itself far outweighed the value of that which it was made to hold. Many boxes made in the seventeenth and eighteenth centuries were decorated by artists who were specialists in painting miniature portraits of those for whom the boxes were made or of notables of the period. This painstaking work is now a lost art as is, indeed, the entire art of making beautiful boxes.

As new materials were developed for the manufacture of furniture, they were also used in the making of boxes. Sometimes this procedure was reversed, as in the case of papier-mâché in England, where trays and boxes were made first and then furniture was produced from this material. The Victorians, who delighted in finding different media that could be adapted to furniture manufacture, made boxes of papier-mâché, pewter, earthenware, tin, silver, and wood and decorated these to look like other materials altogether. Boxes of the same period were designed in shapes that resembled anything but the six-sided containers that had been made in the past. Boxes were made to hold anything that the affluent Victorian might have owned . . . and since he owned a lot, there is a profusion of boxes still available from that period.

If the Victorian lady showed an interest in hand-painting, she must first own a paint box, preferably one made of jasper ware by Wedgwood. If her talents leaned toward embroidery, her sewing equipment must be of the finest quality and enclosed in a magnificent mahogany box, preferably made by a renowned cabinetmaker. If she turned her talents to writing, her paper, ink, and quills would be enclosed in a box that opened to become a small desk. This lap desk could have been made of many different materials and was often magnificently decorated.

Large pieces of Victorian jewelry required large boxes to hold and protect them. Often these boxes were made in interesting shapes,

Snuff box, carved tortoise shell with gold mounts. Eighteenth century.

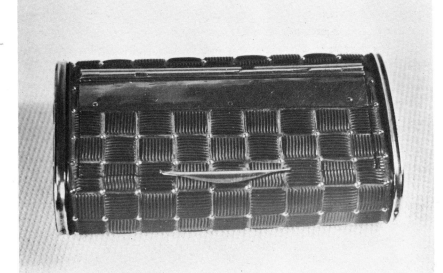

such as houses or castles. If milady traveled, she needed another set of boxes to hold her treasures, for they went with her in the carriage. If her husband felt it necessary at any time to defend her honor, he carried his dueling pistols in a suitably made wood box, with silver or brass fittings, often engraved with his name or initials or family crest so that there would be no question as to whose pistols were whose.

The box has been used to protect, contain, or simply to decorate, for centuries. It has been made of every possible material and in every decorative style in history. Beautiful boxes, perhaps more than any other small decorative antiques, have been preserved and collected. Perhaps the reason for this is that the box, no matter of what material or what size, is functional and practical. Any box that has ever been made will hold something; and even though those *somethings* might have changed or been destroyed down through the years, a well-made box is usually kept. The everyday items of household clutter find their way to a container of some sort, and therefore new uses are found for the box that once held tea or gloves or ink and quills, if the box was attractive and made of a sturdy material.

The old boxes of the past two centuries are now used mainly for decorative purposes. Boxes made lovingly by hand by craftsmen and artists will never again be made in the quality and quantity that they were in the past, nor can any decorative antique add as much warmth and charm to a room as an old wood box fitted with excellent hardware and bearing the patina that only time can give to good wood.

Since boxes have been made throughout the history of the decorative arts, there are boxes to go with any style of home furnishings, for any size room, to suit anyone's taste, and for any practical or impractical purpose. A collection of miniature boxes can become the focal point of a well-decorated room. Often a beautiful box set on a modern table can help create an eclectic atmosphere in a room without the expense of further investment in more costly antiques.

Boxes have been made in the past to contain the various forms of entertainment that families enjoyed together, and a study of these boxes and the things they hold is a study of the history of home entertainment. Boxes have been made for centuries that contained mechanical devices for reproducing music. Games of many countries have survived only because care was given in making the boxes that contained them. Chinese mah-jongg sets, because of the value of the ivory from which they were made, were enclosed in boxes of commensurate value and beauty. Expensive handmade chess, domino, and checker sets have lasted only because their boxes were carefully made. Perhaps it is only fitting that our most modern form of home entertainment, the television set, should be made in the box shape, also.

Whether one's taste in interior design and small decorative accessories runs to the expensive and elaborate or to the simple and primitive, there are collectible boxes to satisfy anyone. Even the most extreme advocate of functional modern design cannot argue the prac-

(Left) *Games have survived intact when their boxes were well made. This mah jongg set was made for an American game manufacturer in China at the beginning of this century. Although not very old, these sets are decorative and, therefore, collectible.* (Right) *Front panel slides open to reveal drawers for tiles.*

(Left) *A great many work boxes of various sizes were made to contain sewing as well as cosmetic equipment. This eighteenth century "necessaire" still contains its original fittings. (Below) Box showing opened top and sewing equipment.*

ticality of the box shape or the decorative value of many of the old wooden boxes. Camphorwood captain's chests, made in China and brought back by the adventurous seamen of the nineteenth century, are used as end tables and coffee tables in functionally decorated rooms. What new pieces of furniture can store as much in as little space, mothproof woolens, and relieve nasal congestion at the same time?

A study of old boxes is a study of man's vices as well as his virtues. Special boxes were made in enormous quantities to hold snuff, tobacco, cigarettes, cigars, playing cards, and dice. On the other hand, the beautiful plain boxes made by the Shakers in the nineteenth century in the United States encouraged neatness and austerity, two admirable qualities that were a part of the Shaker religion.

While much has been written about every type of collectible furniture, pottery, porcelain, and glass, the subject of old boxes as a category for collecting has received little attention in literature about antiques. One reason that boxes have been largely ignored by most writers on collecting is that there is no beginning and no end to a story of boxes. No one book could possibly be a complete treatise

Card cases were an item of the nineteenth century and were made in many materials. The use of the cases has become obsolete but they are now collected as decorative boxes. The above case is of tortoise shell, mother-of-pearl and ivory.

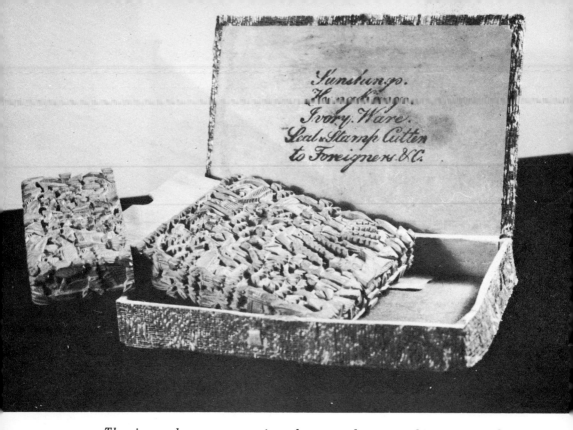

The nineteenth century was a time when many decorative objects were made in the Orient for export to the West. The carved ivory case is in its original silk covered box. Note legend on box is written in English.

on the subject. Boxes have been made all over the world for many centuries in as many materials and combinations of materials. Box decoration can be found that is typical of every age and decorative style known to man. Our purpose here is to acquaint readers with many of the decorative and collectible boxes that are still available, to discuss some of the purposes for which these boxes were made, and in cases where the method of manufacture, decoration, or materials used are not self-evident, to make these methods known.

Because this book has been written primarily for collectors, it would be of little use if all the boxes illustrated were museum specimens. It is all too discouraging for collectors to see only illustrations of museum-owned collections, for while these are usually the best examples in any given category, collectors are all too aware that their chances of finding like objects are quite slim today. It should be encouraging, therefore, for the reader to note that most of the boxes illustrated here are in private collections or the stock of various dealers. Where museum-owned boxes have been used it has been mainly for the sake of convenience rather than the fact that similar boxes can be found nowhere else.

Collectors are always interested in the comparative value of those things that they collect or would like to collect. Some of the boxes illustrated are obviously of great value while others are currently of very little but decorative or historical value. Often there is no logic to the antiques market. For instance, Japanese lacquer, made and decorated by hand and requiring many hours of careful polishing, is often less expensive than the papier-mâché boxes that were manufactured in imitation of it. Yet, only a few years ago, British papier-mâché was held in disdain by antique dealers and collectors alike.

Since no book about boxes can be all encompassing, an attempt has been made in the following chapters to discuss some of the more interesting boxes that are still available for collectors. Where the material, form, and style of decoration or purpose for which the boxes illustrated are not self-evident, these will be explained in the hope that the explanation will further the collector's interest and knowledge. It is also to be desired that the following chapters will encourage the preservation of many boxes that were handmade or hand decorated in the past.

Chapter 2

JAPANESE LACQUER BOXES

THERE are two types of collectible boxes, made in widely separated parts of the world, which have a strong connection with one another. The first is the magnificent lacquer box made in Japan and the second is the papier-mâché box which was manufactured in large quantities in Europe, particularly in England, in the nineteenth century. Good examples of both types can still be found by collectors and both are well worth collecting. Since the papier-mâché industry grew out of an attempt to copy Oriental lacquer decoration, it is important to understand the material and processes involved in making lacquer boxes in Japan.

The art of lacquer work originated in China and goes back many centuries. It is not known exactly when the art became known in Japan, but lacquer ware has been documented in that country since the eighth century. The development of the lacquer process by the Japanese reached an artistic summit in the seventeenth century when it was first introduced to Europeans. Just as all porcelain has been known in the West as "chinaware," so all lacquer ware and the various styles of decoration used to embellish it have been, since the seventeenth century, called "japanning."

Along with its unparalleled beauty, Japanese lacquer ware has other qualities that would have led those Western artisans involved with the manufacture of the applied arts to attempt to discover the secret of its manufacture. Japanese lacquer objects are extremely durable, so that boxes many centuries old will show little or no wear. The finish is heatproof, waterproof, and alcohol resistant. When lacquer was used in the manufacture of cups or plates the

Sweetmeat box is made in two sections with cover. Black lacquer with gold and aventurine decoration.

added qualities of being light in weight and unbreakable made them more desirable than porcelain.

Japanese lacquer is a natural product, derived from the sap of a sumac tree (*Rhus vernicifera*) that grows wild in China but is cultivated in Japan. This sap contains urushi acid, the property that makes Oriental lacquer impervious to water marks and other staining. It is the way in which this raw material was refined, processed, and utilized that remained a secret to the European artists who made numerous vain attempts to copy Japanese lacquer ware.

Most Japanese lacquer boxes were made of a core of white pinewood (*Retinispora obtusa*) which is fine grained and free from knots and resins. The wood was planed to a degree of thinness seldom seen in Western woodwork. Lacquer boxes, therefore, are extremely light in weight. This is the reason that Europeans, attempting to copy the lacquer work of Japan, believed the core to have been made of paper. In rare instances, a core of paper was used by the Japanese. They also used metal and sometimes linen cloth, but pine-wood was used most often.

The finest and most desirable lacquer boxes are those made before the nineteenth century. These are, for today's collector, almost unobtainable, since they have long been sought by museums. The early boxes were often the result of careful work and high artistic skill. One box may have been given as many as fifty coats of lacquer.

11

(Left) *Round lacquer box with silk braid handle on cover. Exterior is gold leaf, lacquered.* (Above) *Opened box showing interior which is red lacquer with pieces of silver and gold foil imbedded in lacquer.*

Small lacquer box has layer of red lacquer over a layer of white. Edges were rubbed so that the underlayer shows through. Gold and bronze floral decoration.

An artist sometimes devoted years to the making and decorating of a single item. By the nineteenth century the industry became large enough, particularly after Japan began large-scale trade with the West in 1859, to necessitate newer and faster methods of manufacture in order to satisfy foreign markets. Since it is these later nineteenth-century and early twentieth-century Japanese lacquer products that are available for collecting today, it is the later method of production that will be of interest here.

In the manufacture of Japanese lacquer, labor and talent were divided into three separate processes, each carried out by three different sets of workmen. Each of these processes required skill, patience, knowledge, and time. The first step involved the extraction and preparation of the lacquer itself. The second step involved the preparation of the article and the application of the lacquer to the prepared article. The third step involved the decoration of the lacquered article. These steps became somewhat shortened by a division of labor, but they still required more time, effort, and talent than can be given to any decorative object to be made in quantity today. The following are the steps required to make a simple lacquer box:

Mahogany color lacquer box in interesting shape. Flower decoration in gold.

The lacquer was extracted from the sumac tree by making an incision in the bark and scraping the inside of the trunk with a spatula-like tool. Once the lac was extracted, it was pressed through layers of cotton cloth in order to remove any impurities, such as pieces of bark or dirt. Exposure to air turned the raw lacquer from a white substance to brown and then to black.

The lacquer was then ground in a wooden tub for the purpose of obtaining a homogeneous liquid. This liquid was again strained and the moisture evaporated from it by exposure to the sun or to artificial heat. During this process, workmen stirred the liquid constantly. Coloring agents were then added, depending upon the type of lacquer required. The colors most often used were aventurine (a kind of copper-brown), cinnabar (an orange-red), black, and chestnut-brown. Two very rare colors are green and white.

After the joiner had painstakingly made the box core of white pine-wood, had filled all joints and crevices and carefully sanded the box to the desired thinness and smoothness, the second step in the lacquering process took place. First the box had to be made ready to take the lacquer. It was prepared with an application of a mixture of rice paste and lacquer, mixed with cotton wadding, which was pasted over all the joints and nail holes to insure further smoothness. This mixture was then dried and all surfaces of the box were spread with

Brown lacquer box made in shape to accommodate unusual decoration on lid.

*Two small lacquer boxes. Left, black lacquer with gold chrysanthemum deco-
ration. Right, dark brown lacquer box holds Japanese hair ornaments which
are also lacquered and decorated. Decoration on box is in relief and is painted
in silver and gold leaf with traces of red. Inner section of box is rust color
lacquer.*

a thin coat of lacquer sizing to fill up the pores of the wood. Then
followed another application of paste, which this time contained
ground pottery as well as the rice paste and lacquer mixture. The application of these first coats was known as "luting." After the second
coat of lute had dried, the box was then polished with fine sandstone.

Following this first polishing, the surfaces of the box were covered
with a layer of Japanese rice paper or thin hemp cloth and this layer
was affixed with a mixture of rice paste and more lac. This process
was done to prevent warping and to give the box tensile strength.
From one to three more coats of the lacquer-paste mixture were then
applied, dried, and rubbed down by hand.

The drying process was done in a damp atmosphere, necessary to
prevent the lacquer from running and drying unevenly. A final prep-
aratory coat of lacquer containing pulverized ochre was then applied, followed by a coat of pure lacquer and often still another coat
of lacquer containing both pulverized ochre and ground pottery. India
ink was then rubbed into the surface and a last coat of black lacquer

might then be applied. The lengthy drying process was necessary between all coats. Finally, the box was rubbed down with a special kind of fine-grained charcoal,

It was only after this long, painstaking preparation that a Japanese lacquer box was ready for the final step, the decoration, which was done by skilled artists. There were, of course, many variations in the preparation of lacquer boxes, one of them being the elimination of the rice paper or hemp cloth so that the grain of the wood showed through the lacquer.

Various forms of decoration were used to embellish Japanese lacquer boxes. One of the earliest known methods of decoration was the sprinkling of gold powder over the lacquer surface and then again lacquering and polishing the box. An aventurine effect was achieved by using gold powder over a russet-brown lacquer ground. Gold foil was used from the beginning of the eighteenth century for lacquer decoration. The foil was arranged by hand in minute squares on the surface of the box, which was again lacquered and polished.

The finest lacquered boxes are those that were artist decorated with hand-paintings of an almost limitless variety of motifs. Landscapes, seascapes, birds, fish, insects, flowers, and animals were used, as well as formal designs of scrolls, arabesques, and diaper patterns. In the hand-painting, gold is always the predominate color, but green, red, blue, and silver appeared as well. All surfaces were decorated on the most important boxes. It it not unusual to see the inside surfaces and the undersides of lids as carefully decorated as the exteriors.

Relief designs were applied to some boxes by the use of a putty foundation which was applied, dried, and then hand-modeled. Metals such as gold, silver, and pewter, as well as mother-of-pearl and ivory, were often applied by chiseling the lacquered surfaces of the box and cutting and inserting the desired shapes from one of these materials and imbedding them into the lac. These inlaid boxes found favor with Europeans and Americans and a great many of them were made for export. The Japanese, themselves, preferred the plain or hand-painted decoration.

Another form of lacquer decoration was accomplished when a cinnabar (red) lacquered box was deeply incised with informal designs, although this type of work was done more effectively by the Chinese than by the Japanese. "Marble" and "tortoise-shell" effects were achieved by the decorator using a mixture of colors and a spe-

Octagonal lacquer box is slate grey lacquer with raised gold painted decoration. Inside is gold spatter decoration. Brass hardware.

Round lacquer sweetmeat box in brownish black lacquer decorated with gold design in allover pattern.

Cinnabar lacquer with carved decoration. Panel set in lid is jade. This box was made in China.

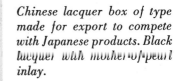

cial polishing process. A type of scratchwork was also used as decoration in which the design was incised in the lacquer and gold foil rubbed into the lines. "Sharkskin" lacquer was made by pressing real sharkskin or the skin of the ray fish into the surface of the box, followed by lacquering and polishing so that the surface was smooth but seemed to have a textured grain.

By 1900 the Japanese lacquer industry was producing articles in enormous quantity for export to Europe and America. Many of these items were extremely elaborate and made only for Western taste. The quality of the lacquer work declined as the demand for things Japanese grew stronger, but the same long process of manufacture was necessary even for some of the inferior work. Eventually, a kind of imitation lacquer work was made that had very little relationship to real lacquer. For this work a kind of lacquer paint was used which had few of the properties of baked lacquer. However, even some of this work had appeal for Westerners who could purchase it for very little.

Among the many kinds of boxes that were made were jewelry boxes, glove boxes, tea caddies, sewing boxes, snuff, cigarette, and tobacco boxes and miniature cabinets. Lacquer connoisseurs and col-

18

lectors in Japan held these Western-influenced articles in contempt and continued to collect only the simply styled and antique lacquer work, although some of the best early lacquer found its way to Europe and America.

While there is little question that the older lacquer is of more artistic merit than that made for the Western market, those methods that were thought in 1900 to have been "modern" and "mass-produced" are today antiquated and painstaking in comparison with any products that are now being made. In 1904 Sadakichi Hartmann wrote of the lacquer industry in *Japanese Art:*

The old artisans, who made beautiful and ingenious things to please the fancy of a daimyo, put good and earnest work into everything they made; but now that the average workmen have abandoned their old unmercenary standard and cater to foreign taste, continually reproducing the same stock of ideas and set of symbols, their productions have become exceedingly bad taste to the connoisseur.

And yet, being after all a good deal superior to any of our factory bric-a-brac, their productions are still able to give us a faint idea of the remarkable imperishable qualities of the art of old Japan.

Eventually, the Japanese lacquer made for export deteriorated in quality and a great number of lacquer objects of this type were exported. Lacquer is painted on and is only a distant relation to the real hand-finished lac.

Chapter 3

BRITISH
PAPIER-MACHE BOXES

As early as the seventeenth century European craftsmen were acquainted with Japanese and Chinese lacquer work and made many attempts to copy it. Since they did not have the necessary raw ingredient for lacquer, they experimented with various varnishes but they were never successful in producing a finish as fine as that of Oriental lacquer. For a while French cabinetmakers compensated for this lack by importing decorated wood panels from the Orient and using these on furniture of their own manufacture and design. There is also evidence that British cabinetmakers sent panels to the Far East to be decorated and lacquered there. The French and English also imported raw lacquer through Dutch traders, but since they

Papier-mâché box, hand-painted and gilded. Painting signed at bottom, "Broad-beck." Early nineteenth century.

Group of papier-mâché snuff boxes, painted and printed decoration.

were not fully aware of the methods of application, this attempt at copying was not entirely successful.

"Japanning," an attempt of British manufacturers to imitate the Japanese lacquer process and the Oriental style of decoration, was first used on ironware in the eighteenth century. Iron was found to be rather unsuccessful as a base for the British varnish, and tinware was soon substituted. The Pontypool Japan Works was founded by Edward Allgood in 1730 for the purpose of making this Oriental-style decorated tinware. All tinware of this type became known as "Pontypool."

In 1740 John Baskerville opened a japanned-tinware factory in Birmingham and soon after began to experiment with molded paper pulp as an alternative to tin for japanning decoration. Another type of paper product was devised by Stephen Bedford and John Taylor, which consisted of paper sheets pasted together. Stephen Bedford also experimented with varnishes in order to compete for a prize offered by the British Society of Arts in 1757 to anyone who could approximate the work of the Martin Brothers of France.

The Martins developed a copy of Japanese lacquer before 1730 that closely resembled the quality of the imported lacquer. They

21

were able to make their varnish in many colors and their work was highly successful. The Martins were granted a monopoly on japanned work in France, and their secret was so closely guarded that it died with them. *Vernis Martin* boxes are the finest of all European lacquer boxes.

By 1763 Stephen Bedford was awarded half the prize for inventing a varnish that one might assume was half as good as the Martin brothers'. Bedford's varnish was used on compressed paper panels, although by this time he is said to have preferred papier-mâché. The problem of discovering a proper surface in order to approximate Japanese lacquer work and the results of this experimentation led to the growth of a large lucrative industry in Great Britain, which lasted through most of the nineteenth century.

Papier-mâché was first used by the English in the seventeenth century as a material for applied, carved, or molded decoration. This first composition was made of plaster mixed with hay, straw, and other vegetable matter. It was usually made in the form of slabs and then carved. At about the same time a form of mashed paper was being made on the Continent and eventually this type of material became popular for various uses in England. In the eighteenth century Robert Adam used papier-mâché for his neoclassic architectural decorations on ceilings and interior walls. These decorations had the advantage of being very light in weight. Therefore, they were easy to apply and they could be uniformly prefabricated. Adam's decorations were made of paper pulp mixed with chalk and sand, which was then pressed into molds and baked.

By 1770 the manufacture of papier-mâché was firmly established in Birmingham, England, which became the center for manufacturing and decorating this product. In 1772 Henry Clay invented a heat-resisting paperware that, once processed, had all the properties of wood. Heretofore, in England, papier-mâché had been molded or carved into the necessary shapes. Clay's invention revolutionized the paperware industry in that now all manner of objects could be made from this material, which could be sawed, dovetailed, nailed, carved, and sanded just like wood. It also had the added advantage of taking the newly developed japanned decoration better than any other product that had yet been found.

From the beginning of the nineteenth century decorated papier-mâché products, the first of which were tea trays, were manufactured in quantity in Birmingham. Wolverhampton became a second center

Papier-mâché letter file, black with tinted mother - of - pearl decoration and red and gold hand painting. Marked: Jennens and Bettridge.

Japanned spectacle case with mother-of-pearl and pewter inlay decoration. Pearl shell is tinted and laid in mosaic patterned border.

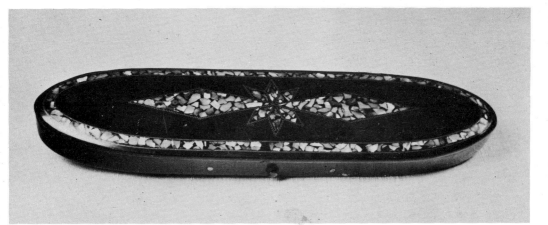

for the japanning trade. Many new items were made including, eventually, furniture. However, boxes of many shapes, sizes, varieties, and uses were a large part of the industry's output. Because boxes do not ordinarily get the same amount of use and wear that larger pieces of furniture do, there are still many boxes of papier-mâché available to the collector. Many of these are still in very good condition. The variety made include tea caddies, boxes for writing, snuff, and games

23

Papier-mâché snuff box with silver inlay border and traces of tinsel decoration in center.

Papier-mâché jewel box, molded shape. Black with all-over painted decoration in gold leaf and overpainted in red and green. Center panel once held reverse painting on glass for which manufacturer, Lane, was noted. Damaged panel has been replaced with watercolor and glass panel.

boxes, as well as many others that may have had no specific function other than that they would hold *something* and were decorative.

The variety and quality of decoration used in British papier-mâché work in the nineteenth century are of interest to the collector because it was the ability of this product to take japanned decoration that led to the success of the entire industry in England. Eventually, lack of taste in the decoration led to the industry's demise.

Artists, hired to devise new methods of painting, varnishing, and inlaying papier-mâché articles, became specialists in applying various motifs. One man, for instance, painted only parrots while another specialized in painting peacocks. Papier-mâché lent itself to hand-decorating and the exotic designs and techniques that became fashionable at the height of the Victorian era. Many methods of decorating paperware products were devised, and all innovations were displayed at the exhibitions that were popular all over Europe in that century.

The most important development in papier-mâché decoration was the invention of a lacquer finish which, while not as durable nor as attractive as the Japanese lacquer it was made to imitate, was at least an improvement over earlier British japanned products. The firm of Jennens and Bettridge, makers of the best quality British papier-mâché, developed a finish that required numerous bakings and hand-polishing and pumicing. This was a comparatively expensive process, even at a time when cheap female and child labor kept costs down. Jennens and Bettridge spared no effort to produce a paperware product that was superior. The company was established in 1816 and in 1825 was designated "Makers to the Queen."

Articles made by Jennens and Bettridge are usually marked, but if not, the quality of the lacquer work, smooth and satiny to the touch, and the restraint of form and decoration, unlike much of the cheaper and more garish articles made at the height of Victoria's reign, make the best work outstanding enough to be identified as that of this singular company. Jennens and Bettridge hired well-known artists to decorate their products with hand-painted motifs and to devise new, and to the Western market unique, methods of decorating, many of which had already been used by the Japanese.

The earliest motifs that were painted on British papier-mâché boxes were Oriental scenes or scenes of British life. Shell decoration later became popular for tops of boxes and other flat surfaces. Since the British decorators were familiar with Japanese lacquer work, they attempted to copy all the techniques used by the Japanese, but being unaware of the methods used, they had to devise their own. They experimented with their own techniques for inlaying and decorating. Philip Alsager and George Neville, former apprentices at Jennens and Bettridge, started their own firm in 1846 and together these two men developed a form of papier-mâché decoration whereby thin layers of sea shells were applied in designs of butterflies and flowers and the

(Above) *Papier-mâché tea caddy. Bronze color with hand painting. Marked: Jennens and Bettridge.* (Below) *Interior of tea caddy which is decorated with ivory.*

lacquer was built up around these applied designs so that the shell appears to be inlaid or imbedded.

The shell that was used for inlay was the inner layer of the nautilus, which is hard and iridescent. The first shells were used in their natural color, the designs being obtained by employing various cross sections. This method of decoration was quickly taken up by other firms, and soon the shells were tinted or painted and used with other forms of decoration such as hand-painting or metal inlay. Some papier-mâché firms made only undecorated forms, which were then purchased and decorated by companies that specialized in that aspect of manufacture.

Because shell decoration became the major means of embellishing boxes and other things made of British papier-mâché, it is necessary that the collector be aware of the processes involved. It is often possible to tell by the quality of the applied decoration the age and relative value of a box he might wish to purchase.

The first shell designs were cut by hand from very thin layers of the inside of the nautilus shell. The layers were further thinned by hand-polishing, grinding, and pumicing. The desired patterns, most often flower motifs, were then applied with varnish to the surface of the already lacquered object. Many layers of varnish were then added to bring the surface even with the shell decoration. The varnish covering the shells was then polished away, giving the impression that the design had been inlaid rather than applied. After further polishing, a box was often embellished with hand-painting or gilding.

As shell decoration became the most popular form of papier-mâché decoration, simpler methods of applying the mother-of-pearl were devised so that the decorating could be done on an assembly-line basis. However, there was no way to avoid a certain amount of hand labor. Stamping machines were used to cut many layers of shell at a time. These layers were glued together to facilitate the stamping process and then the glue was washed away, leaving many individual, but identical, shapes for the decorators to use.

Boxes decorated in mother-of-pearl can still be found. They will vary enormously in quality, but it does not require the knowledge of an expert to recognize the best of these. Jennens and Bettridge and a few other companies made many boxes on which the pearl shell decoration is delicately tinted and on which the design has depth and artistic restraint.

Other forms of decoration used were the Oriental scenes already

Papier-mâché compendium, hand-painted and gilded with mother-of-pearl inlay in castle scenes.

(Below) *Compendium showing top panel and drawers opened. Original shiny quality of lacquer is seen in places where there was no exposure to light.*

Heavily decorated papier-mâché compendium. Front shows borders of mosaic-style mother-of-pearl inlay in pastel-tinted colors. Flowers are also mother-of-pearl inlay with overpainting.

(Above) Compendium opened to reveal carved pearl shell spool holders and sewing equipment. Panel in lid is pin cushion made of satin which is embossed in gold. Seven drawers hold writing and sewing equipment or jewelry. Bottom section, which is removable, is a lap desk.

Papier-mâché lap desk with pearl shell and painted decoration.

mentioned. This kind of decoration, executed in gold powder, is sometimes mistaken for Japanese work by those who are unaware of the difference in quality between real lacquer and the British varnish. Although one was made in imitation of the other, there is little similarity between British papier-mâché and Japanese lacquer. Papier-mâché is thicker, less refined, and the best finish does not compare with the Japanese lacquer. Oriental motifs were often used in the eighteenth century for European decoration in the applied arts.

Various types of inlaid panels were devised expressly for the decoration of papier-mâché boxes. A pearl shell decoration behind glass was used, as well as a kind of reverse painting on glass employing the use of ground gem stones, colored glass, and foils instead of paint. Jennens and Bettridge also used Wedgwood cameos as decoration. These were imbedded in a manner similar to the shells.

The early boxes, those with hand-painted scenes on the lids and hand-gilded borders, are highly desirable as decorative accessories and examples of the best work in papier-mâché. As well as hand-decorating, lithographed pictures and transfer prints were applied to the lids of boxes and varnished over. These examples of early color printing are also in demand now.

By 1850 the English papier-mâché industry was at its height and some of its production was exported to America. Probably a great many "blanks" were sent here for decoration, also, although there is the possibility that many of the boxes printed or painted with

30

American motifs were decorated in England. Many of the lids, particularly those on snuff-boxes, have varnished lithographs of color portraits of American patriots. It seems probable that they were printed in America and sent to England for application.

The industry began to decline toward the end of the century and was almost nonexistent by 1900. By this time there was a craze for things Japanese and lacquer ware imported from Japan was a superior product. It was probably much cheaper, too. The overdecorated styles of the Victorian period and progressive mechanization of the papier-mâché industry led to the manufacture of cheapened and bizarre items which did not long remain in favor. Many glittering items were relegated to the attic, barn, or basement, and it is only within the past ten years that the decorative value of papier-mâché has become appreciated once again. Everything, from simple, well-used snuffboxes to elaborate combination workboxes and writing boxes, is now avidly sought by collectors. Removed from the clutter of the Victorian parlor, papier-mâché has come into its own once again.

Chapter 4

AMERICAN, RUSSIAN, AND GERMAN LACQUER BOXES

A LTHOUGH by far the greatest amount of papier-mâché "japanned" work that is found today was made in the two towns of Birmingham and Wolverhampton in England, artistically successful work was done in other parts of Europe, and for a short while in at least one town in America.

Papier-mâché was produced between the years 1850 and 1854 by the Litchfield Manufacturing Company of Litchfield, Connecticut. Previous to this time, the same firm was engaged in the manufacture of daguerreotype cases and the metal inserts that were used in them. However, poor working conditions in the papier-mâché industry in England led skilled workers to emigrate to America in the thirties and many of them settled in Litchfield. Their knowledge of the paperware industry and the methods of decorating this ware were put to use by their new employers.

Due to the proximity of Litchfield to what was at the time the center of the clock-making industry in America, a great many papier-mâché clockcases were produced in Litchfield, although some boxes and other items were also produced. The only items that seem to have been marked were the clockcases, and therefore it is difficult to identify work done in Litchfield. The quality of design and decoration is quite as good as British work. Pearl shell decoration was used as well as hand-painting and gilding. The quality of the American varnish leaves a lot to be desired by papier-mâché devotees, however. The surface of Litchfield varnish is not smooth as it should be, and the long periods of hand-polishing and pumicing do not seem to have been employed in the finishing of the work. This would seem an inevitability in a town that had a relatively small population and where there could not have been enough cheap labor to perform this long and arduous task.

Regardless of the quality of the varnish, the decoration of paper-ware articles made at Litchfield is quite successful. A motif often used is the single rose of tinted mother-of-pearl and hand-painted foliage and other embellishments. However, there was nothing unique in this decoration. It was very like the work done in England.

After only a few short years, the Litchfield Manufacturing Company merged with a clock-making firm in Bridgeport, Connecticut, and gave up the manufacture of papier-mâché for this more profitable product for which that state had already become famous.

The later papier-mâché boxes found in America, decorated with engravings of American subjects, are most likely of British manufacture. It is probable that the prints were sent to England for application, although it is more likely that the blanks were sent over and the boxes were decorated and varnished in America.

While attempts to reproduce Japanese and Chinese lacquer led to French, English, and German boxes being made for that method of decoration, it is not generally known that very successful lacquer

Russian lacquer box, hand-painted and signed by the artist.

(Left) Russian lacquer tea box, tin lined. Decoration is hand-painted. (Right) Underlid of box showing mark.

work was made in Russia dating back to the eighteenth century and the time of Peter the Great. It is also not generally known that this work is still carried on in Russia in a successful attempt to preserve this folk art. The towns of Palekh and Fedoskino are the two centers where the industry is still in existence.

Characteristics of Russian lacquer work are the excellent quality of the lacquer and the painted or polychrome decoration. The material used is papier-mâché. The lacquer grounds used are black or imitation tortoise-shell, and many coats are applied in a long and painstaking process not unlike the methods first used in the eighteenth century. Decorated snuffboxes, made in Fedoskino (formerly Danilkovo) in great quantities in the early nineteenth century by Piotr Vasielievich Lukutin, are probably the finest of all old Russian lacquer boxes but are also extremely rare today. Lukutin's boxes were very durable and the processes he employed in producing a perfect material for his lacquer work from compressed sheets of cardboard were lengthy and painstaking. Evidently Lukutin realized that the success of "japanning" depended upon the quality of the papier-mâché itself. His boxes were given numerous coatings of lacquer with laborious hand-polishing between the applications. A fine patina was obtained by first soaking the boxes in vegetable oil and hardening them in low-heat ovens for a long period of time.

The earliest Lukutin boxes were decorated with themes similar to those used by the English and German decorators. Landscapes and skylines as well as genre subjects were used. Some boxes were decorated with pearl shell decoration as well. Toward the middle of the nineteenth century Russian folk motifs were used. This type of decoration continues today.

34

The Lukutin family continued to run the business successfully until it closed in 1904. From 1828 on, the products were marked with the Imperial eagle and the various initials of the members of the family in charge of the factory at the time.

The styles of decorations of paper workboxes in Palekh differ from those decorated at the old Lukutin works. In 1917 some of the artists and craftsmen of the lacquer industry formed cooperatives and revived the art before it became lost. Many of the icon painters of pre-Revolutionary days began work in Palekh decorating lacquer boxes. Painted in egg tempera rather than the oils used in Fedoskino, the Palekh style is fanciful and somewhat less realistic than the Fedoskino scenes. Palekh lacquered boxes are highly prized and might well be the highest quality and best decorated of any papier-mâché boxes available today.

Lacquer work was produced in Germany in some quantity in the eighteenth century also. However, in the field of artistically decorated boxes, the name of one man stands out. This was Johann Heinrich Stobwasser, who settled in Brunswick in 1763 and opened a small shop for the production of decorated lacquer products. Stobwasser learned lacquering from the producers of paperware in Ansbach who made military items and some cheaply decorated com-

Russian lacquer box of type made in Fedorskino.

mercial products. Stobwasser improved on the Ansbach method of decoration and produced artistically decorated lacquer ware.

Tin, wood, and papier-mâché were used by Stobwasser for lacquer decoration. He made pipes, mugs, cups, trays, table tops, and other pieces of furniture, but the products for which he is best remembered are his japanned snuffboxes. To the confusion of devotees of papier-mâché snuffboxes, copies of English prints were used as decoration for the tops of the snuffboxes. Battle scenes, copies of old master paintings, and portraits of contemporary figures, as well as historical and fictional characters, decorated the tops of Stobwasser's boxes. These German-made boxes can be identified by their shape, which is usually oval or round with concave side rims. The art work is always of the best quality and the mountings are plain, in keeping with eighteenth-century neoclassic style.

Stobwasser snuffboxes are usually marked on the inside of the lid with a print of a horse over "St." or the full name of the firm. Some

Trinket box made of turned wood and hand-painted in Russian folk motif. Decoration is black, yellow and red on silver ground. Marked: Made in USSR (Russia).

Silver cigarette box, hand lacquered in enamel colors on red. Troika scene. Moscow, Circa 1880.

of the Stobwasser snuffboxes are unique in that he allowed his artists to decorate the under side of the lids with erotic paintings.

Stobwasser retired from business in 1810 and his son carried on production until 1832, when he sold out and moved to Berlin, only to begin again in the same business. The original Stobwasser firm continued under different management until the beginning of this century. A great many Stobwasser boxes were exported, and because of the excellent quality of the work, it was as desirable as the best British japanned, decorated paperware.

Today's collector, searching for Russian, American, French, or German papier-mâché snuffboxes or decorated papier-mâché boxes other than British will find these in rather short supply. The Stobwasser boxes, because many of them are signed, are very desirable. *Vernis Martin* boxes have always been revered by collectors because the work is of such superior quality. The decorated Russian boxes are charming enough to have found their way into collections over a long time, and the later production that is still being carried on has not been exported yet in any quantity, but the new Palekh boxes already have become very desirable to collectors.

Chapter 5

SNUFFBOXES AND
SOUTH STAFFORDSHIRE
ENAMELS

THE general subject of miniature boxes can not be treated sufficiently in one very large volume, let alone one chapter. However, since these tiny delights have become the most desirable of all boxes for collectors and connoisseurs, it is necessary to acquaint readers with the purposes for which miniature boxes have been made in the past, the materials used in making them, and the manner in which these materials were decorated. Hopefully, the information given will aid the collector in identifying specimens, the time in which they were made, and their countries of origin.

Once made in enormous quantity, miniature boxes are now eagerly sought and collected. Many have great value and others can be purchased at present for very little investment. Often collectors of tiny old boxes limit their collections in one way or another; either by the material from which they were made, style of decoration, historic interest, or often simply by the relative value of the boxes themselves. Most frequently, however, miniature boxes are purchased by the collector for their aesthetic appeal. Many of these boxes fall into the category of jewelry and were made by jewelers from precious and semiprecious materials and painstakingly decorated. They were meant to be worn or carried on the person and were, at the time of their use, admired as fine jewelry.

Vernis Martin snuff box. Top is lacquered tortoise shell and sides and bottom are green lacquer. All outside surface, including bottom, are hand decorated and gilded. Box is made of pressed horn. French, circa 1755.

Pressed horn and tortoise shell snuff box. Shape and materials are very similar to Vernis Martin box.

Although many date back to the seventeenth century, they were not collected until the middle of the nineteenth century. Their original functions became obsolete and except for those made out of valuable material or inset with precious of semiprecious stones, they were neglected, and many were broken or lost. However, in modern society the more decorative of these boxes have found a definite function which no seventeenth-century aristocrat could have foreseen. For our pill-taking society, old miniature boxes have become a convenient and functional means of carrying the pills, capsules, and artificial sweeteners that seem to represent our own time in history. One is not apt to feel quite so sick if his medication is safely in his pocket enclosed in a George III snuffbox made of solid silver with diaper and quatrefoil motifs engraved. Nor is one apt to feel quite so

Tortoise shell and silver snuff box. Eighteenth century.

(Below) Enameled snuff box, hand-painted and gilded. Borders surrounding cartouche are rose-pink. British, eighteenth century.

(Below) Two copper enameled snuff boxes made in England. Left, motto box, "My love is pure and will endure." Right, hand-painted snuff box with sepia color decoration.

deprived if her sugar substitute is served in a Battersea enamel box decorated by hand with tiny flower motifs. While the original purposes for which these boxes were made may be long forgotten, new uses have made them once again the luxurious accessories to dress that they once were. We no longer wear these little boxes on chatelaines at the waist or around our necks on chains, but they do fit easily into pocket or purse and are once again brought out and compared and admired over after-dinner coffee.

The majority of the smallest decorative boxes were made for two purposes, to hold snuff and to carry scent to ward off or mask offensive odors. The value and beauty of a snuffbox represented the station and importance of its owner in the eighteenth century. There were small boxes made for many purposes other than keeping snuff, although it is safe to say that the majority of the small boxes collected today were made for that one purpose.

The European habit of "taking snuff" (tobacco which has been fermented, dried, and then ground to a fine powder and flavored) is said to go back to the days of Columbus who, as legend has it, found the Carib Indians using it. In the seventeenth century, Louis XIII introduced the use of fancy snuffboxes to his court. The possession of elaborate and valuable snuffboxes became the pride of every seventeenth- and eighteenth-century aristocrat. Limoges enamel snuffboxes date back even further than Louis's reign.

For the European aristocracy, snuff-taking became a ceremony requiring definite and studied movements of the hand and wrist which required careful learning. Classes were held in London in the eighteenth century for the purpose of teaching the proper methods of administering snuff. An important part of this "ceremony" was the possession and proper display of a suitably decorative snuffbox.

The snuff habit was not limited to men only. As late as the nineteenth century in America, Dolley Madison, wife of the fourth president of the United States, carried her own gold and enamel snuffbox and often offered it to visiting statesmen during moments of stressful conversation.

At various times in the history of snuff-taking, attempts were made by rulers to squelch what many thought to be a harmful and dangerous habit. The Victorian rigidity of the latter half of the nineteenth century finally accomplished what heads of state had been unable to do. Sniffing snuff became a pleasurable habit that the middle and lower classes could afford, and therefore it went out of favor for the

Two enameled snuff boxes from South Staffordshire region of England. "Hat"
opens at bottom as does the other box.

Delft comfit box for carrying sweetmeats in pocket or purse is enameled copper. Circa 1850.

aristocracy. Those hooked on the habit used snuff privately. Among the working class the use of snuff prevailed in the wood-built factories of the nineteenth century where smoking was not permitted.

No longer a product that is openly advertised as are other tobacco products, snuff is still produced and sold in surprisingly large quantities, particularly in America. A great portion of the snuff that is produced is sold privately to consumers by mail order. Therefore, it is safe to assume that many early and beautiful snuffboxes continue to fulfill the function for which they were originally made, albeit less flamboyantly.

A decline in the public use of snuff was followed by a decline in the production and quality of the little boxes that were made to hold it. The most collectible and valuable snuffboxes are those made in the seventeenth and eighteenth century for display in the "snuff-taking ceremony" by the aristocrats. Less expensive and less highly decorated snuffboxes fulfilled the needs of the nineteenth-century working class very nicely. Today we collect all snuffboxes including, even, the boxes in which snuff was originally packaged.

Fancy snuffboxes, made in every possible material from which

Enameled and hand decorated snuff box. Restoration on front panel. Of South Staffordshire manufacture.

boxes could be made and decorated with meticulous care by the European artists and craftsmen of the seventeenth and eighteenth centuries, are now avidly collected. All snuffboxes had to be made with a certain amount of care and precision because snuff, a substance affected by exposure to moisture, had to be kept in airtight containers. The first requisite of a carefully made snuffbox was a perfectly fitting cover.

Among the most collectible of all miniature boxes are those that were made in the South Staffordshire region of England. These boxes are porcelain enameled on copper, and the most highly prized and priced are those decorated in rococo style and made at Battersea. These boxes are important because many of them are examples of the earliest transfer printing on porcelain. True Battersea boxes are extremely scarce and it has become commonplace for collectors to call all copper enameled boxes of the eighteenth century "Battersea," when in truth very few of them are. The Battersea factory was in existence for only six years (1750 to 1756) and similar work was done to a much larger extent at Bilston, Birmingham, and Liverpool. Any boxes made and decorated in the neoclassic style of the late eighteenth century are most definitely not from the Battersea factory.

Nineteenth-century collectors realized the artistic and historic value of Battersea boxes, and Lady Charlotte Schreiber, an avid British collector of that century, described in her posthumously printed diary the often futile search for Battersea boxes. Lady Schreiber's passion for collecting took her all over the Continent in search of British ceramics. It is ironic that her collection, now in the Victoria and Albert Museum, has been said by scholars to contain a good deal of work that is not from the Battersea factory at all but are later

Snuff box. Silver with polished jade insert in cover. Birmingham, 1898.

French snuff box. Silver with tortoise shell inlay in cover. Circa 1800.

(Right) Etui, *or needle case. Battersea-Bilston type enamel with silver gilt mounts. These small cases held sewing equipment and other necessities and were hung from chatelaines at waist.*

fakes and boxes made in other factories. If Lady Schreiber, a completely obsessed, knowledgeable, and dedicated collector, had a difficult time finding and identifying those precious boxes in her day, we can rest assured that a good deal of the so-called Battersea boxes offered for sale today are fakes or reproductions.

An American collector and author also cited the scarcity of these Battersea boxes in the nineteenth century. Writing in *CHINA COLLECTING IN AMERICA,* published in 1892, Alice Morse Earle lamented: "A few snuff-boxes of Battersea enamel still remain to show us how lovely they were, but the frail china ones have nearly all been destroyed, and when still existing are usually sadly cracked and disfigured." Miss Earle also states that "china snuff boxes were offered for sale in the *Boston Evening Post* of April 16, 1773, were bought and filled with Kippen's snuff, were lost in Boston streets, were advertised for reward in Boston papers, and no doubt proudly and ostentatiously carried by Boston beaux."

The earliest enameled snuffboxes were made by jewelers from gold and could be owned only by the wealthiest snuff-sniffers. Copper enameling was a less expensive copy of the technique used on

45

Ivory bodkin case. Wedgwood medallions set with silver gilt mounts.

(Left) *Silver snuff box, embossed decoration. Eighteenth century.*

these earliest boxes and these copies were made to satisfy a less affluent market. Opaque white enamel was fused to the thin copper core, which was first hammered into convex shapes by hand. When metal casting dies were developed in the late eigtheenth century, more elaborate shapes were formed.

The earliest copper-enameled boxes made in England were made almost entirely by hand. After the thin copper had been hammered into the desired shapes, white enamel was spread over their surfaces by means of a spatulalike tool. Later a method was devised whereby the copper parts could be dipped. This speeded the production of these boxes, for which there was a great demand. The frames were made in Birmingham, a region that later became the center for papier-mâché manufacture.

Methods for decoration of enameled boxes changed as England also became geared to mass production at the turn of the century. At first each color in the decoration was applied by hand by the decorator. The fact that they are hand decorated is what makes the earliest boxes so desirable to connoisseurs. When transfer printing was developed by John Brooks, who worked at Battersea, the enameled boxes could be decorated more quickly and less skill was required. Many boxes were printed in black with scenes and portraits and then color was applied over the outline by hand. This technique did not require great artistic skill. Eventually, printed decoration without the overpainting was used. Mottoes, sayings, and inscriptions were printed on many of these later enameled boxes. Of these, the boxes with colored grounds, rather than white, are the most rare, and therefore the most desired by collectors.

Besides snuffboxes, which comprised the largest portion of this type of manufacture, patch boxes, comfit boxes, miniature sewing boxes, and pillboxes were made. Since true Battersea boxes are seldom seen for sale today, collectors now seek the later enameled boxes which are, after all, the result of that combination of mass manufacturing and handwork that has also become a thing of the past. At present, even the nineteenth-century reproductions are desirable collector's items.

Chapter 6

FRENCH AND
FABERGE BOXES

THE rococo style Battersea boxes were, after all, only an imitation of the finer and more costly enameled gold boxes that were made by the French goldsmiths in the seventeenth and eighteenth centuries. The French had been and continued to be the style-setters in the decorative arts. They gave as much care and attention to the manufacture of boxes as they did to the design and fabrication of their magnificent furniture. The styles of the boxes made closely follow the various changes in the style of French interior design.

The probability of finding French-made boxes today is not as remote as one might think. Although the miniature boxes have been collected continually since they were first made, there are magnificent larger boxes, often incorporating several of the materials and furniture-making techniques for which French cabinetmakers are famous. Detail, design, and workmanship on many of these boxes are unsurpassed, and although they are apt to be quite costly, French-made boxes of any of the decorative periods are the finest the box collector can own.

Among the most beautiful boxes made in France were those that incorporated the techniques and materials used by André Boulle in

French jewel casket. Tortoise shell veneer over wood. Etched rock crystal panel in cover and cut velvet lining in red. Bronze doré mounts. This type of veneer in the manner of Boulle enjoyed a renaissance in the nineteenth century. (Below) View of above box showing cover and lining.

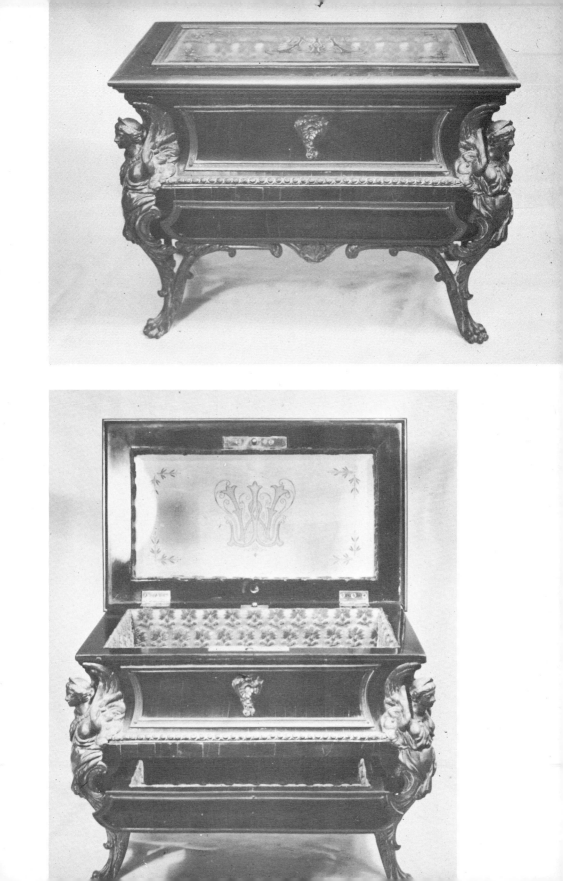

Perfume box, made in France. Cut rock crystal and silver gilt. Fitted with original crystal bottles and funnels made of silver gilt. Circa 1825.

the late seventeenth century. Tortoise-shell veneer inlaid with brass in marquetry patterns adapted well to box shapes. Many of this style of box were further embellished with ormolu mounts. Porcelain medallions made at Sèvres can be found on old French boxes, as can lacquered paintings on panels. Wood and wood veneers, carefully inlaid in intricate patterns, are the adornment on many French boxes. Ivory and brass inlay, magnificently styled, decorate even some of the most utilitarian boxes of the Louis XVI period. Decorative French boxes for perfumes, cosmetics, sewing and writing equipment can sometimes be found.

There are many boxes made by the *art nouveau* glassmakers in Nancy at the turn of the century, and while these are eagerly sought by collectors of cameo glass, one of these boxes, particularly one made by Emile Gallé, would be a find for any box collector.

A type of miniature box that is collected today and may be somewhat more plentiful than the desirable snuffboxes is the vinaigrette. Vinegar hardly seems a condiment worthy of the tiniest of decorative boxes that were made, but it was discovered rather early that sponges soaked in vinegar were an aid in warding off or masking putrid odors. During the latter half of the eighteenth century and the first half of the nineteenth century, miniature boxes were made of silver, silver gilt, and many of the other materials from which snuffboxes were made, that could contain small bits of pungent sponges. Often, scents of rosemary, mint, lemon, or spices were added to improve on the vinegar odor. It is probably even more likely that perfume was used on the sponges in these tiny boxes that hung from chatelaines at the waist along with other bibelots. Vinaigrettes have hinged grids that fit under the lids of the boxes to hold the damp sponge in place.

(Left) *Ebony decanter box. Ivory, brass inlay.* (Right) *Burl walnut decanter box. Gutta percha panels. Circa 1880.*

Necessaire *with original fittings. Red tooled leather, fittings are silver gilt. Made in France for export. 1840.*

(Left) *Silver* nielloed *box, Russian. Architectural scenes on lid.* (Right) *Underside of silver box showing match strike.*

Polished agate case for ciga-rettes. Clasp is gold set with rose diamonds and star sap-phire. French, late nineteenth century.

Most of the vinaigrettes to be found today are silver and were made in England. Often they can be found in fanciful shapes other than the conventional box shape. Particularly charming are the vinaigrettes made in purse shapes, watch-case shapes, book shapes, and fish and animal shapes. French vinaigrettes are not as plentiful as are the English silver vinaigrettes, simply because many were made of materials more valuable than silver and have been collected longer. Of particular interest to collectors of these most miniature of all boxes is the pierced work on the inner grids, which is usually in keeping with the exterior design and decoration of the box.

French boxmakers and jewelers also used their talents in making patch boxes to hold the cloth patches that were used as early as the sixteenth century as a form of facial adornment. In the seventeenth century the wearing of patches, cut into fanciful shapes such as stars, half-moons, crescents, diamonds, squares, and more ambitious sil-houettes, became the accepted fashion for the aristocracy. Patch boxes, or *boîte-à-mouche,* usually have a small mirror set inside the lid, and since they were made for the aristocracy, they, too, were made of precious metals and set with gems or enameled.

Etuis (miniature sewing kits to hang from chatelaines), *néces-saires* (a larger sewing kit), rouge boxes, toothpick cases, comfit boxes, and needlecases are all examples of the French jeweler's art. These were made of a variety of materials and were always beauti-fully decorated.

There is such a variety of decorative styles and materials used for the making of boxes by the imaginative French craftsmen throughout

53

Silver cigarette case decorated with various enameled crests. Hinged section at end is for match storage and match strike. Russian, circa 1900.

the past centuries that the subject can only be touched on here. Those fortunate collectors who own even one good French box have the satisfaction of knowing that it is of excellent design and taste. Chances are, too, if it was hand-crafted, that it is the only one exactly like it in the world.

Since French art styles spread so rapidly throughout the Continent, there are many boxes of European origin other than French that closely resemble the boxes from which they were copied. Since so few boxes were signed by their makers or marked with their countries of origin, there is usually no way to discover where they were made. Only boxes made in distinctive national styles or from materials native only to one region are simple to identify.

Boxes made of precious material and decorated by hand are categorized as "objects de vertu." These usually belong to the category of fine jewelry and while most of this type of work was done in the seventeenth and eighteenth centuries, there is one man who worked at the end of the nineteenth century with precious materials. Since his work is so outstanding and was made in enough quantity as to be still available, although expensive, he deserves some attention here.

54

(Left) *Russian silver cigarette case with art nouveau motif embossed. Late nineteenth century.*

(Right) *Enameled silver stamp box. Signed by H. Wigstrom, Fabergé workmaster. Pale blue enamel with garlands of flowers in eighteenth century style.*

(Left) *Fabergé box in a Fabergé box. This enameled cigarette case is lilac color on gold with diamonds as decoration. It is the work of Michael C. Perchin, Fabergé workmaster. Circa 1900.*

55

Russian enameled silver casket. Signed by Fedor I. Ruckert, Fabergé work-
master.

Peter Carl Fabergé was a Russian descended from a Huguenot family who revived the art of enameling in transluscent colors on silver and gold. Fabergé worked in Russia in the last quarter of the nineteenth century and was in charge of a factory that at its peak employed five hundred artists and craftsmen. Fabergé designed, decorated, and closely supervised the manufacture of many "objects de vertu" from clocks to automata, but the largest category of his firm's production was boxes.

Many boxes were designed and made with raised work on silver or gold. This raised work was carefully designed expressly for the applied decoration in enamel that is associated with Fabergé's workshop. Careful integration of design on the part of the metalworkers and the enamelers resulted in exquisitely designed boxes that are unsurpassed for their decoration and workmanship.

Working at a time when the guilds produced art work of hand-made and·individually designed quality in a manner first proposed in the nineteenth century by William Morris in England, Fabergé's firm turned out magnificent objects from precious metals and stones. In opposition to William Morris's idea in nineteenth-century England that the handmade should, through the group cooperation of the guild, be available to the masses in order to upgrade their taste in decorative objects, Fabergé's art then, as now, was for the very rich. Fabergé's art style, especially evident in his enameled and jeweled boxes, was unique in that it combined both the traditional Russian folk motifs with the *art nouveau* motifs that were popular at that time.

The quality of the engineering design of Fabergé's boxes should also be noticed, for it was perfectly contrived. Hinges and clasps all work with precision. Many of the boxes conceal complicated automata that are delightful. All work done by Fabergé's guild is now in demand by collectors, although this was not always so. Many collectors of more traditional silverwork held the bright colors of the enameling somewhat in disdain until ten or fifteen years ago. Fabergé's work is now recognized as a superb example of an art style that is typically Russian.

(Right) *Russian enameled silver casket. Made in Moscow by the eleventh Artel. Circa 1900.*

(Below) *Enameled cigarette case signed by Fedor I. Ruckert, Fabergé workmaster.*

Silver snuff box, enameled. Made in Russia, circa 1900.

Since Fabergé's production was hardly of a type that appealed to Russian revolutionists, Fabergé went into exile in Switzerland when his factory was closed and he died there in 1920. An interesting mark that appears on one of the cigarette cases illustrated in this chapter tells something of the history of what happened to art treasures during this period of turmoil in Russia. As the Soviet leaders planned for industrialization they found that they were sorely in need of foreign currency. Several stores were opened in Moscow to sell Russian art treasures and booty taken from collections of the nobility and rich bourgeoisie. This cigarette case, made by Fabergé's firm before his exile, is marked also with the stamp of the Soviets. It was probably sold in one of these "Torgsin" stores.

(Opposite top) *Cigarette case, Russian enameled silver with swan motif. Mark indicates that case was made in the Fabergé workshops before Russian Revolution, but added Soviet mark tells that case was sold after that period.*
(Bottom) *Russian enamel snuff box with lily of the valley motif on cover.*

59

Chapter 7

KNIFE BOXES AND VENEERED WOOD

Beautiful woods and wood grains were recognized and appreciated for their beauty early in the history of furniture manufacture. Veneering, the process of gluing thinly cut layers of precious wood to surfaces of less exotic wood, goes back to ancient times and became popular during the Renaissance, when inlay designs and intarsia were common forms of furniture decoration. At this time there were no known methods of cutting large enough slabs of wood to the desired thinness in order to cover entire surfaces with single sheets of the more precious wood. Therefore, small pieces of wood were cut and glued to the carcass of a piece of furniture in patterns and designs that took advantage of the beauty of the wood grain and variations in color.

By the seventeenth century, veneering became an art, and the decorative use of thin sheets of wood can be found on many existing examples of European furniture dating from that period. The French were the style-setters in marquetry inlay, and British and other European craftsmen soon followed suit.

The advantages of using thin sheets of wood to cover another kind of wood are, perhaps, obvious. However, it might be well to investigate them here because there were so many boxes made that would not have survived in such excellent condition nor would they have been so beautiful were it not for the development of commercial wood-veneering. The first advantage to consider in the veneer process is the reduction in cost of a veneered surface of an exotic and

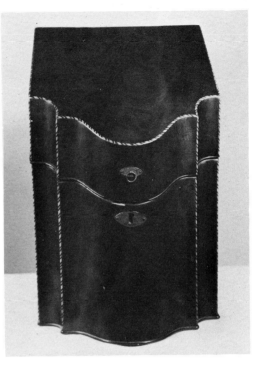

Mahogany knife box, one of a pair, with rope-carved edges and curved front. Circa 1800.

expensive wood that is applied to a less expensive domestic wood. Second, another practical advantage is that the tensile strength of a surface is increased many times when the veneer is laid cross grain to the under piece of wood. The additional feature of a layer of glue between the two surfaces also adds to the strength of the finished product.

The aesthetic advantages of the use of veneers in the decoration of cabinetry are increased, also. The maker, by using thinly cut sheets of the same piece of wood, can repeat the grainings and markings in order to form interesting patterns. This use of the natural design in wood required artistry as well as craftsmanship. By using veneers judiciously, the maker could inlay designs and decorations of different kinds and colors of wood, thus producing interesting motifs and styles.

Before the nineteenth century, veneers were cut by hand by specially trained veneer cutters who were highly skilled in slicing the layers of expensive wood to uniform thickness. These sheets were then sold to furniture makers and boxmakers, who used them in decorating the many kinds and styles of decorative furniture and boxes that developed in the seventeenth and eighteenth centuries.

At the beginning of the nineteenth century a steam-driven saw was registered in London that made it cheaper, faster, and easier to cut large, thin, uniform slices of wood to be used for veneers. It is probably safe to assume that a good many of the existing veneered boxes are of nineteenth-century production. After the special saw was invented, wood was cut in many different ways to take advantage of the variations in grainings.

The different designs that can be obtained in veneered wood depend on the type of wood used and the way in which the log is cut. The earliest methods of cutting veneers by hand produced only the vertically cut grains. This vertical slicing achieves a pattern which is circular and is known as "oystering." Other types of graining commonly used in the nineteenth century are "crotch," cut from the area of the tree where two limbs fork out, the "burl," a growth on the tree trunk and a particularly attractive gnarled design, and "bird's-eye," which is formed by the deep growth of buds most commonly found on the maple tree. Many other patterns can be obtained by the expert cutting of the wood in different cross sections and the employment of the saw in cutting circular sections around the log.

Woods often used in veneer are chestnut, poplar, walnut, elm, birch, rosewood, primavera, ebony, satinwood, sandalwood, sycamore, box, yew, olive, pear, teak, tulipwood, laurel, and many other similar exotic woods. Mahogany was and still is the most popular veneer wood. It is strong and hard and has figurations in the various cuts of its grain that are unmatchable for their beauty. Mahogany also takes a high polish extremely well. Because of its lasting popularity, it is becoming scarce.

A large variety of boxes was made of veneered wood in the nineteenth century. British boxmakers, especially, turned out a great many veneered boxes. All of these are avidly sought by collectors today, but perhaps the most beautiful of all veneered boxes made in England are knife cases.

Articles of great rarity and value have historically been encased in boxes of comparative artistic value. Often, elaborate boxes were made to protect valuables against damage, and more often, theft. Sometimes elegant boxes were made simply as a means of displaying that which they contained to its best advantage. Such must have been the case with the slant front and urn-shaped boxes made to hold

French ebony perfume box with brass inlay, carved beaded edge on lid. Original glass bottles are gilded. Watered crimson silk lining.

horsehide into which small seeds were pressed. The leather was then dried out and soaked. The impression of the seeds, after they had been removed, swelled up and made an interesting textured pattern on a leather that took dye easily. The color most often used for shagreen was, not surprisingly, green, although red dye was sometimes used. The deal carcasses of the boxes were covered with shagreen, and often silver fittings were made and placed at the corners of the box where there would be the most wear. Other kinds of leather were used, and tooled leather can be found on early knife cases.

In the latter part of the eighteenth century, knife cases were designed and made in the Hepplewhite and Sheraton styles with slant fronts, hinged lids, and beautiful veneered surfaces. Urn-shaped cases in the style of Robert Adam became a popular adornment on neoclassic style sideboards. The neoclassic revival and the subsequent designs applied to interior decoration led to the repeated use of the classic urn shape. Knife cases were made of wood veneer that were copies of Grecian urns, round and tall with covers that were attached to a center rod and could be raised and lowered. These

Collar box of veneered woods showing magnificent graining and inlay. Drawers are deep and rounded to hold stiff collars.

urn-shaped cases were made in pairs or sets of three with a smaller case for spoons.

The manufacture of veneered knife boxes was a complicated process since the curved surfaces of both types presented special problems. Once the boxes were contoured it was necessary to treat the veneer with heated sizing so that it would conform to the curves without splitting. The deal carcass was thinly coated with glue, which was then allowed to dry. After the veneer had been soaked in size it was pressed to the deal with the use of a heated, inverted form of the contour shape. The whole was then clamped tightly together to press out the excess size and glue and to allow the veneer to adhere and harden onto the deal. The outside form was then removed. Flat surfaces of veneer were applied by the utilization of a veneer hammer.

Final staining and polishing and several waxings by hand finished the outside of the knife box. The interiors of knife boxes were carefully made, also. Partitions for the knives, which were set in vertically, handles up, were covered in felt or velvet and the undersides of the lids were also lined. With the addition of hardware and mountings of silver or brass, the boxes were finished. Some knife boxes were veneered on the inside and many of these boxes have marquetry borders on the interior which match those on the outside.

Motifs in veneered inlay were used as restrained decoration on the Hepplewhite and Sheraton knife boxes. The conch shell and the Prince of Wales plumes are two motifs that are seen often. Veneer motifs were made and sold separately to boxmakers, who would then inlay the motif during the veneering process.

Many boxes were made using veneered woods, once the power-driven saw was developed. Those with contoured lines presented somewhat more of a problem than the more simple boxes. Sewing compendiums, cases for liquor bottles, and many other boxes were made, all of which are eagerly sought today.

CANISTERS, CHESTS
AND TEA CADDIES

ALTHOUGH tea drinking is said to have been a custom in China from about 2700 B.C., it was not introduced to the Western world until the early seventeenth century. The first shipments of tea to England and the Colonies date around 1650. Due to its long journey and its rarity in England in the seventeenth and eighteenth centuries, tea was expensive and therefore rated commensurate containers in which to keep it.

Partaking of tea was, in eighteenth-century England, a ritual that has carried over into this century. However, as the ritual changed and the price of tea became lower, the containers in which the tea was kept changed also. The earliest containers for tea were bottle shaped and were made of porcelain, pottery, tin, or silver. As tea drinking became more ceremonious, boxes were made to hold these containers, whose shape changed to accommodate the space of the box. Therefore, the bottles became square containers and the mouths of the containers were widened so that the tea could be scooped out rather than poured as before. Glass and silver were the materials most often used for these tea canisters, which fitted into the box that was made to keep the precious tea fresh and safe from pilferage.

Eventually, the tea canister became unnecessary and the box itself became the container. These boxes were lined in lead foil and had one, two, and less frequently, three sections. The double-section box is the one most frequently found. It held two different varieties of tea leaves, which were blended at the tea table in the proportions

(Left) *Enameled copper tea canister, Battersea type. Sepia color hand-painted decoration. Circa 1755.* (Right) *Wedgwood creamware canister, printed decoration in black. Circa 1760.*

most favored by the lady of the house. The double partition box had loose-fitting inner covers, and the box itself could be locked. This box became known as a tea caddy after the Maylayan word "kati," a standard weight for a package of tea weighing one and one-third pounds. The fact that tea caddies were made to accommodate this weight accounts for their all being approximately the same size.

Eighteenth- and nineteenth-century tea caddies have become very collectible, their value being ascertained by the elaborateness of style, quality of workmanship, and desirability of the material used in making them. The earlier boxes that were made to hold the separate containers filled with tea are, technically, tea chests rather than caddies. Many of them look, indeed, like small chests or traveling trunks.

The earliest tea chests were made of deal and covered in tooled leather with silver mounts. These were followed by chests covered in shagreen and chests made of mahogany and walnut. As wood veneering became easier due to the development of the steam-driven saw, wood tea chests were veneered and inlaid in many kinds of exotic wood.

Tea chests and tea caddies were made in all the styles that re-

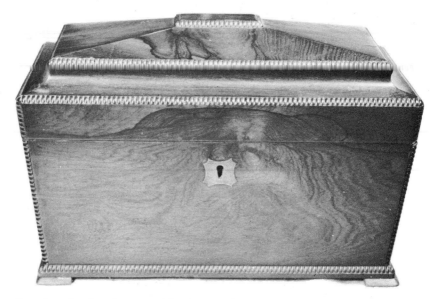

Tea chest fitted with removable silver canisters.

Tea caddy, embossed tortoise shell with ivory trim.

Interior of tea caddy.

Tortoise shell tea caddy with silver escutcheons and ivory trim. Circa 1820.
(Below) *Interior of tea caddy. Cover lined in velvet.*

Papier mâché tea caddy with mother - of - pearl and hand-painted decoration.

Original printed paper lines the lid. Lead foil in lining in compartments.

flected a century and a half of the development of the British decorative arts. The early elaborate boxes were heavily carved wood in the rococo style of the early eighteenth century. The Chippendale influence of the middle eighteenth century was responsible for boxes

Sheffield silver tea caddy. Early nineteenth century.

with heavy ormolu mounts and hardware and Oriental-style decoration. Later in the century we find lighter, more classic styles influenced by Adam, Hepplewhite, and Sheraton. The woods used in these boxes were those that are lighter in color and weight. At this time the classic shapes and style of decoration dominated all objects for the home. The use of veneer led to inlaid decorations of scrolls, shells, sprays of flowers, and wreaths, as well as the classic acanthus or diaper borders that were adapted from the Greek and Roman artifacts.

Boxmakers of the nineteenth century experimented with many different materials for decoration. These materials were mainly applied, in the manner of veneer, over a carcass of wood. Tortoiseshell was very popular from the turn of the century until about 1820. It was used in thin sheets that were glued over the deal. The shell was used either plain and polished or embossed. Ivory, either plain or carved, was also used at about the same time. Mother-of-pearl inlay was used for decoration of many boxes, the later examples being etched with designs, crests, or monograms. Sheffield plated silver was also used for tea caddies. In short, just about every material that could be made into a box or used for its decoration was adapted by the boxmakers who created containers for tea. The more attractive of these are now sought and collected simply as decorative boxes. Since so many were made in such a variety of materials and styles of decoration, there are tea caddies that appeal to every box collector and it is possible to specialize further in tortoise-shell, papier-mâché, or other kinds of tea caddies.

Perhaps the most collectible tea caddies are the fruit-shaped boxes of the late eighteenth and early nineteenth centuries. These caddies were made of wood in the shapes of pears, melons, apples, etc. Silver handles, in replicas of stems, were used as decoration. These caddies, filled with tea, were popular gift items of the time. Because of their great popularity as collectible boxes, there are few seen for sale today, and when an important collection is offered at auction, the prices are usually high.

Carved wood Bible box, American. Late seventeenth century.

Chapter 9

WRITING BOXES
AND COMPENDIUMS

THE original writing or desk box dates as far back as the history of writing. A box in which writing materials were kept, called a *scriptorium,* was in use by monks during the Middle Ages. These boxes were eventually mounted on stands and later legs were added. These became the ancestors of all desks and the use of the writing box survived into the nineteenth century. The Gothic boxes had lift-up lids that were hinged in the back. The tops were either flat or slanted toward the front to provide both storage inside and a writing surface when closed. Most of the earliest desk boxes were made for ecclesiastical purposes rather than domestic use.

After the desk boxes were mounted on stands and given legs, drawers were added and desks in many styles were designed. However, the utility of an easily portable box to provide storage for writing materials and a surface on which one could write led to the continuation of domestic usage of a smaller and more compact box that became very popular in the eighteenth century. Lap desks were also made in some quantity during the nineteenth century. Many of these later boxes were made of decorated papier-mâché.

The major advantage of the writing box that became popular in the eighteenth century was, of course, that each individual could have his own place in which to keep his letters and papers and writing materials. Ink, quills, paper, sand, wax wafers, and seals were all necessary equipment one used in writing a letter. Writing boxes were quite portable so that they could be held on the lap or used at

Writing box, veneered wood
with mother-of-pearl escutcheons. Box has removable tray
in top and fold down writing
surface covered in green velvet with embossed border.
Lid lining is green satin.

Above box in open position.
Circa 1850.

Lap desk with brass inlay, ebony wood. Slant front folds down making ample writing surface. Space in back for ink wells and storage space for paper in bottom of box.

a table. In days when central heating was unheard of, members of a family could gather close to a fire and each work at his own small desk.

Many magnificent wood and wood-veneer writing boxes were made. These are perfect examples of utilitarian design and were contrived to take advantage of every inch of space contained within. The majority of these writing boxes are made somewhat alike in that the top opens up to reveal a removable compartment tray for storing inkwells, pens, sand, seals, and wax. Under the tray is a hinged and folded surface for writing which, when opened, provides ample space for the writer to work. These writing surfaces were often covered in cut velvet, felt, or tooled leather. A bottom compartment, under the lid, provides space for storing papers and letters.

The form of writing box described above is the most usual, but there are many variations of writing boxes that were made. There are smaller lap desks with lids that slant upward toward the back. These lids are hinged at the front and open to form a writing surface with only one compartment underneath for storage.

Veneered wood compendium with silver fittings. Front drawer opens to reveal fold out writing surface. Secret drawer is inside of box. Dated: February, 1875.

Small workbox with pewter and mother-of-pearl inlay. Silk damask lining.

Writing boxes were made of many materials and since they were in use for such a long period of time they can be found in many decorative and national styles. The most highly prized desk or writing box in America is the one made of pine or oak in the William and Mary style that was in use from the time of the first settlers. As well as holding writing materials and paper, this box was the place where important documents and the family Bible were stored. Many Bible boxes were decorated with simple carved motifs which sometimes included the initials of the owner and the date the box was made.

The most elaborate nineteenth-century writing boxes are those that combine storage for painting, make-up, and writing utensils, with space for jewelry and other small valuables. Although these compendiums finally superceded the small writing box or lap desk, they are masterpieces of utilization of storage space and design. Many have secret drawers that were probably a secret to no one, and some are hardly portable at all. These larger, all-purpose chests have some of the charm and appeal that an old dollhouse would. The most elaborate are those made of papier-mâché and are painted, gilded, and inlaid.

Made in the days when ladies and gentlemen (wisely or unwisely) kept detailed diaries and wrote many letters, the writing box enjoyed a wide popularity. Today the telephone, typewriter, and ball-

Wood veneer work box of art nouveau design. Circa 1900.

point pen have made the functional qualities of writing boxes obsolete, but as decorative boxes they are more sought after than ever. There is a certain romance in writing boxes of the past centuries. One can picture many romantic novelists and poets using just such a box while working close to the fire.

Chapter 10

TRUNKS AND CHESTS

THROUGHOUT the history of civilization the one form of furniture that has never changed much is the storage chest or trunk. Man's first form of furniture, the chest served as chair, bed and table. From early times its primary purpose was, of course, the moving and storing of clothing and household articles. The first chests were small and portable, but as people became settled in one place for longer periods of time, the chests became larger. Eventually, drawers were added as well as legs and many different furniture forms evolved. However, the original box-shaped, hinged-lid chest continued throughout the centuries to be a practical method of storage. Chests have always been made in the various woods indigenous to their countries of origin, and from the time of the early Romans and Egyptians chests have been decorated by artists and craftsmen in representative national styles.

While our concern here is mainly with smaller boxes, it is necessary for the collector to understand that many of the eighteenth- and nineteenth-century boxes to which we are attracted today are the descendants of these early trunks and chests. As people began to gather more of the accouterments of living, and dress became elaborate, special boxes for traveling were made to hold specific things. Many of these small chests were fitted with bottles, jars, sewing equipment, writing utensils, and even complete porcelain tea services. Today, these traveling chests are in demand by collectors who appreciate the historic as well as artistic and decorative value of these fitted chests. With the popularity of air travel we now carry as little as possible when making a journey as opposed to the Vic-

Travel trunk, hide covered with copper hardware and brass nailheads. Late eighteenth century. (Below) Label under lid describes other wares made for export to America by London firm.

HENRY MILLER,
TRUNK & PLATE-CASE MAKER
(FROM LONDON)
No. 312, Pearl-Street, facing Peck-Slip, New-York.

Makes and sells, wholesale and retail, all sorts of Hair and Brass-mounted Travelling Trunks, such as Post-Chaise Trunks, Flat and Spanish Sumpters, Hair and Black Leather Portmanteaus, Chaise-Seat Trunks, and small do. to go under the seats of Coaches, Ladies Hat-Boxes, and Fancy Morocco Leather-Work Trunks. Merchants supplied with all sorts of Nests of Trunks for the East and West Indies. Bridle Cases, Camp Trunks, and Travelling do. Whole Leather Trunks to go behind Chariots, and other do. the top of Coaches.

... of persons at sea, in case of Ship...

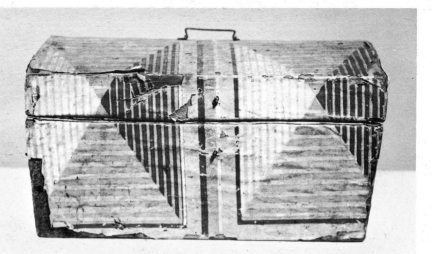

Small dome-topped trunk. Wood covered with paper. Possibly child's or doll's trunk. Early nineteenth century American.

torian, who seemed to have taken with him everything he owned.

Many of the larger traveling chests have great decorative value today. Old trunks, hatboxes, seamen's chests, blanket chests, and even miniature doll's trunks are avidly sought today by collectors who appreciate the value and beauty of hand-wrought brass or iron hinges, lock escutcheons, and strapwork. Many of these old trunks are lined with old newspapers that are of interest to collectors and historians.

Since today's collector is not apt to come across a fifteenth-century Italian cassone or even an authenticated American-pine blanket chest, we will confine ourselves here to those chests and trunks that are still available, albeit in dwindling numbers, and that are currently enjoying a vogue among decorators and interior designers. Most of the available larger chests and trunks are of nineteenth-century origin and while no one collects them in number, they are currently being resurrected from attics and basements and those in passable condition are being restored and used as furniture.

Perhaps the most sought after of all the nineteenth-century storage chests is the seaman's, or captain's, chest. These chests were made in many sizes, often of camphorwood, and were brought back from the Orient by the sailors of clipper ships. They were used on board ship for storage and so many have survived because they were heav-

Hat box covered in hand-painted paper. Early nineteenth century.

ily and sturdily built to withstand rough crossings and a lot of use. Their current popularity has been due to the fact that they are of a furniture style that is timeless. The wood, when cleaned, refinished, and lacquered, is a warm honey color with beautiful graining. Brass corner hardware, handles, and locks are of a quality that has stood up well. As is true of all boxes, these chests are practical as well as being of a furniture style that blends well with modern decoration. Captain's chests are currently being used as coffee tables and benches and have become so popular that they are being copied and mass-produced by modern furniture manufacturers.

There are many other Oriental chests that are always in demand as decorative accessories. Lacquer chests, usually of the nineteenth century, can sometimes be purchased. Many of these have dome-shaped lids and are, therefore, not as practical as furniture as are the camphorwood chests. However, they do make attractive storage furniture and are used in bedrooms for extra blankets and in children's rooms as toy chests.

It is unlikely that the early settlers to America brought more possessions with them than they could carry in the small wooden chests that were used as luggage in those days. Later trunks, made in America, were fashioned after these imported chests and were made of wood or leather or a combination of both. These were used for storing linens and other household goods. It is from these that the later travel trunks evolved that were also leather-covered wood with hand-forged iron hardware. The earliest handmade American trunks were small in size but by the nineteenth century they had grown to very large proportions to accommodate the elaborate wardrobes and accessories of that period. Brass nailheads often adorned these later chests. In the mid-nineteenth century trunks with domed lids became popular when Jenny Lind traveled through the country with luggage of similar shape.

Since many of these early trunks made historic trips across the American continent, there are more available in the Western part of the country for the collector than there are in the East. Although

(Right) Doctor's box fitted with drug bottles. Mahogany with brass fittings. Circa 1830.

Camphorwood sailor's chest made in Singapore. Brass hardware and double locks. Circa 1835.

Glove box covered in celluloid paper which is printed and embossed to resemble enameled ivory. Circa 1890.

they are becoming scarce, they are sometimes used as accessories with primitive-style American furniture. They are examples of early American craftsmanship that are of historic importance. It is usually difficult to date these trunks with any certainty, although where newspaper was used for lining them it is sometimes possible to find a date that way.

A more practical kind of American storage box for linens and blankets that is often found today is the pine blanket chest. These large boxes with hinged tops are primitive in style but almost all of those offered for sale today are of the late nineteenth century or are copies of early New England chests made of old wood. Since they were so useful for storing blankets they were made and used in the rural areas of New England well into this century, and any novice collector should be extremely wary about paying a high price for one of these.

Dower boxes, chests of soft wood, usually pine, were made in Pennsylvania soon after the first Swiss and German settlers became established in that area. Hand-painted motifs in peasant style were used as decoration on these storage chests and many of them bore the names of the women for whom they were made. Some of these chests were signed by their makers. The authenticated Pennsylvania dower chests are eagerly sought by regional museums in that state The collector should beware of recently painted old chests that are sometimes offered by auctioneers in the Pennsylvania region and represented as original old decorated dower chests. It is not likely that many truly old and authentic Pennsylvania dower chests will come on the market today and if they do the competition for their purchase will be very strong.

Other types of Pennsylvania chests were made of oak and were hand carved. Some of these are more refined in workmanship and detail than the painted chests. Oak is easier to work than some of the softer woods. These old chests were made primarily for the storage of extra bedding. When one considers that fabrics were hand woven and hand embroidered, it is no wonder that some effort was put into the manufacture and design of the chests in which they were to be stored.

Set of handmade dominoes might not have survived were they not kept in original sturdy wood box with lock. American, circa 1850.

Chapter 11

SHAKER BOXES OF AMERICA

PERHAPS the most beautiful of American unadorned boxes are those made by the Shaker sect in the late eighteenth and throughout the nineteenth centuries. To understand something about these boxes and why they are so desirable for collectors of Americana, it is necessary to understand something of the Shaker sect, itself, for Shaker craftsmanship is a direct outgrowth of the Shaker philosophy and religion.

The Shakers were a religious society begun in England by its founder, Mother Ann Lee, who emigrated to America in 1774 with seven of her followers. They settled in a community near Albany, New York, and spread their beliefs until there were, eventually, eighteen Shaker communities in New York, New England, and west to Kentucky, Ohio, and Indiana. The philosophy of the Shakers was seen in the communal type of living and working together in these celibate communities. Extraneous decoration in the home and dress were forbidden. The Shakers occupied themselves in the hand-crafting of furniture and boxes in which function, utility, and craftsmanship were the principle features of manufacture. They felt that their work was "Godly" and therefore should be as perfect as possible, both in materials used and in utility. Extreme neatness, cleanliness, and hard work were tenets of the Shaker religion that governed their everyday lives. Their reward was in the satisfaction of the work itself, which they believed to be divinely inspired.

The Shakers' belief that "beauty rests on utility" was the force that led them to make simple, carefully constructed, and utilitarian furniture. Many of the communities supported themselves by selling

Group of three Shaker boxes. The two largest are varnished while smallest is painted yellow.

this furniture to the "outside world." Whether made for sale or for their own use in their communal homes and meeting houses, the same perfection and simplicity of style prevailed.

Because of their divinely ordained neatness ("Clean your room well; for good spirits will not live where there is dirt"), there was a great need in the communal homes of the Shakers for boxes in which to keep the few possessions they had.

"Provide places for your things, so that you may know where to find them at any time, day or night," was another teaching of Mother Ann Lee. The Shaker boxes were made in many sizes and were a part of the necessary furniture in rooms where none of the appurtenances of daily life were exposed to dust. Just as the furniture styles made by the Shakers are plain and primitive of line, so are the boxes primitive and functional. What makes Shaker boxes stand out among other wood utilitarian boxes of the period is the quality of the workmanship and honesty of design and use of materials.

The boxes most commonly associated with the Shakers are oval storage boxes with carefully fitted removable lids. These boxes were most often made in nests of three and fitted perfectly one inside the other. They are usually made of maplewood, which was cut into thin

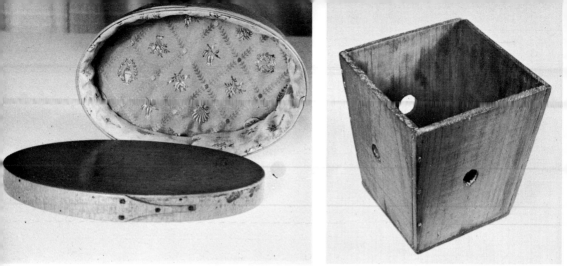

(Left) *Shaker box is lined in silk to be used as sewing box.* (Right) *Shaker berry box. These were made to fit into larger box to facilitate carrying and storing. Holes are for ventilation.*

strips with fingers that lapped over the side seam. The wood was wrapped around an oval mold and permanently shaped through the use of steam. The lap-over fingers of wood were attached over the seam by the use of handmade iron or copper rivets. Pine was the wood most frequently used for the bottoms and tops of the Shaker boxes, Most of these boxes were carefully sanded and varnished, but homemade paint in red, blue, yellow, and green colors was also used.

While these nests of boxes are not very different in style from utilitarian wood boxes that were made elsewhere in America at the same time, the boxes made by the Shakers are easily discernible by the quality of the workmanship evident in them. The lap-over style of joining also distinguishes Shaker boxes from others of the same general style. Finish and patina of these carefully made boxes illustrate that as much care was given in the finishing of each box as was given to important cabinetwork, at which Shaker artisans were also adept. Oval and round boxes were made for sale to the outside world throughout the nineteenth century and at the beginning of this century, although Shakers have now dwindled in number to be almost nonexistent.

Other Shaker boxes, less easily found today, are desirable both to collectors of Americana and to collectors of small decorative antiques. Most of these more rare boxes were made strictly for the use of the Shaker communities. Berry boxes, some of them still bearing stains from the juice of blueberries or strawberries, were made of maple in an inverted truncated pyramid shape. These boxes have ventilation holes in the sides and bottom and were used in a larger, square, shallow box or tray into which they fit snugly for carrying and storing. Even these berry boxes, made for such a mundane purpose, are precisely made and finished. Shallow boxes for growing seedlings and larger boxes for carrying and storing vegetables were also made in quantity. Various kinds of household storage boxes were also made: candle boxes, sewing boxes, dustboxes, pipe boxes, woodboxes, and other utilitarian boxes are all evidence of the Shakers' passion for neatness.

Boxes were made by the Shakers after about 1850 that were used as commercial packaging for the goods that they either made or grew to sell in order to support their communities. Small boxes of wood were made to hold their dried herbs and seeds. These were labeled and are now collectors' items, for they, also, were made with careful attention to details.

Any of the old American-made wood boxes, Shaker or not, are sought today for collections. Many of these still bear traces of the old homemade vegetables dyes that were used as paint. Round wooden boxes, made for the storage of bulk foods in country kitchens, are particularly in demand, for they are an indication of how our forefathers lived in the early days. They, as well as the Shaker boxes, are examples of a type of design and craftsmanship that has disappeared.

(Right) *Small round box made of wood painted blue.*

(Below) *Maple wood bucket with wire handle. Used in American country kitchens for storing bulk foods. Circa 1870.*

Chapter 12

AMERICAN STORE AND COUNTRY BOXES

IT is difficult to imagine why many old boxes that we collect and prize highly today were ever saved in the first place. At the time when the first American store boxes were made, they had as much value to the owner as an empty tin can would have for us today. We can be grateful, however, that there are always people who are born hoarders of seemingly useless objects, because the old boxes that were used for commercial packaging are now known to be of artistic and historic importance.

One of the first designers of engraved trade labels was Paul Revere, who is noted for more important accomplishments. By the beginning of the nineteenth century, product identification had become an important facet of American business. One of the first American products to have been packaged in an identifiable manner was Durham tobacco, which was uniformly packaged following the Civil War. While it is true that before this time some handmade articles were signed by the craftsmen who made them, this was not generally the rule and there was no identification or standard of quality of the goods sold in bulk by peddlars or in general stores. Merchandise that was not standardized or trademarked created a problem for consumers and merchants alike. Merchants often had their names stenciled on their boxes in an attempt at store identification and advertising. These early wood boxes, many of them handmade, are very desirable for collectors of Americana.

Tobacco, beauty preparations, medicines, soaps, candy, and spices

(Left) *Storage box of maple wood with handcarved hinges on handle. Circa 1850. American.*

(Right) *Maple pipe box. Drawer at bottom is for storing tobacco. Eighteenth century American.*

(Below left) *Tin document box. Hand painted in colors of yellow, blue and red on black varnish. Brass handle.* (Right) *Old tin store box. Few have survived to trace history of nineteenth century commerce in America.*

(Above) *Old wood store box still contains original bottles and contents. Early printed labels.* (Top right) *Old tobacco tins were among the most colorful of early store boxes.* (Center right) *Wood box with label.*

(Below) *Match boxes with colorful printed labels are all collectible today.*

were among the first products to be packaged and labeled. In some cases the boxes and jars were imported for domestic products. Bear's grease made by Felix Pratt was put up in pottery jars made by Wedgwood. Other pottery boxes were later imported from Japan. As each industry developed in America, boxes and labels were designed for packaging and identifying the products, and these early packages are avidly sought by collectors. Many of the early nineteenth-century wooden, tin, or pottery boxes in which came snuff, soaps, ginger, and other exotic spices cost the manufacturer or importer very little. Now these packages, long emptied of that which they contained, have value many times what the original product cost. With the growth in number of small regional museums in America, their curators search for examples of the first packages representing the industries of their area.

Collar boxes made of turned wood were used for stiff collars made by Goodyear or Beecher. Matchboxes, cookie boxes, pasteboard shoe boxes, and decorated paper-covered hatboxes are sought. Decorative tin boxes that once held biscuits made in England are collected on both sides of the Atlantic. Many of these boxes were kept because they were both decorative and practical and served other purposes once their contents were consumed.

It is not just the early boxes that are sought by collectors. Even though the paper bag was invented by the middle of the nineteenth century, special boxes for luxury goods were made by hand until much later. Jeweler's boxes, made in Philadelphia from about 1840 until around 1920, are collectible because they required a great deal of handwork in their manufacture. Made on a pasteboard base and covered with velvet or other fabric, the sections for these boxes were formed by steaming the pasteboard on a form to obtain the dome tops. The fabrics for the covering and the lining were glued in by hand and the entire process was time-consuming and required skilled craftsmen. Currently, these small and not very old boxes have become almost as valuable as the jewelry they once contained.

Other utilitarian American boxes that are in demand today are the wooden boxes of the early German craftsmen of Pennsylvania. Of all American country boxes these are by far the most decorative. Made of pine, walnut, or maple, these boxes have either hinged or removable lids and the earliest were dovetailed and pegged. The later boxes were put together with nails.

Made for many purposes, the Pennsylvania boxes are found in

Gift box of nineteenth century has engraved print on cover. Made in shape of book entitled, "Young Lady's Present."

many shapes and sizes. There are candle boxes, knife boxes, spice boxes, and boxes that were placed on chests of drawers and that are often categorized, for want of a better term, as trinket boxes. Oval "bride's boxes" have also been found, although many of these have been documented to have been made in Germany. The painted or scratched decorations on many of the early Pennsylvania-made boxes are similar in style and motif to the boxes that were imported at the same time. This peasant style of decoration consists mainly of brightly painted flowers, such as tulips or morning glories. Spatter paint was also used in the decoration of these boxes.

The folk art of the German craftsmen of Pennsylvania has been revived often and therefore the collecting of any of this work is extremely risky today unless the collector is aware that he is very apt to purchase a box that is typical of the art but probably not very old. Because the Pennsylvania folk-art style is one of the few truly regional styles of folk decoration to have developed in America, prime examples have long been sought by regional museums.

Originally painted in bright colors, many of the early Pennsylvania boxes have faded into soft, muted tones. The collector should remember that it is not difficult to obtain the same faded shades and the "old look" on newly made boxes.

Any wooden boxes that are examples of the work of the early craftsmen in America are in demand today. Round or oval boxes were made in New England and sold in sizes ranging from tiny pillboxes to covered boxes as large as twenty-four inches in diameter. These were used as containers for all the foodstuffs that were grown locally and stored for the winter or for holding the bulk foods that were sold in stores. Many of these boxes were sold by itinerant peddlars in the early days.

The major problem for the collector of early American woodenware is that of deciding what it truly "early." There is no way of dating many of these country items, although it is sometimes possible to tell whether a utilitarian box has some age or not. Wooden boxes of this simple style were made and used well into the nineteenth century. Since they are no longer being made, except by a few craftsmen who reproduce them as accessories for Colonial style decoration, they are quite collectible if they have any age at all. Therefore, they are in short supply and when put together with handmade rivets are quite desirable. Any example of an early hand-crafted container of wood, particularly those that were painted with homemade paint (usually red or blue), would be a "find" today for the collector of Americana.

Another kind of box that is sought by American collectors is the toleware document box. These boxes were styled after the japanned

Box containing child's game has brightly printed self-explanatory cover.

Tin box, probably for cookies or crackers, with copy of painting of U. S. Frigate "Constitution" by Clifford W. Ashley (original in art gallery, Canajoharie, New York). Decorative box has no advertising. Circa 1920.

(Right) *Small tin trunk once held Russian tea. Embossed and printed motifs are typically art nouveau in style.*

(Left) *Many old boxes of little value are kept out of sentiment. This paper covered wood box once held French perfume. 1921.*

tinware of the English manufacturers and it is often impossible to tell whether some of them are, indeed, British, or whether they were made by American tinsmiths, many of whom were British in any case. The earliest examples of American tinware were undecorated, but the boxes most apt to be found today are of a later variety and were painted with asphaltum varnish and then decorated by hand with designs in bright colors. These document boxes were made between 1750 and 1850. The later boxes have stenciled designs, which was a faster, easier method than hand-decorating. Most families owned at least one of these tin boxes in which they kept important papers and money. There are, of course, more to be found of the stenciled variety, particularly in the New England and upper New York State areas. The name of the family to whom a particular box belonged is often stenciled on the lid.

The early tinware trade of America was centered in New England, with the largest amounts being produced in Connecticut and Maine. Trinket boxes were made that were decorated with designs taken from nature, such as flowers, trees, animals, and birds, as well as

Fancy store boxes and two jewelry boxes. Paper and velvet covered and satin lined. These boxes were made in Philadelphia and required a lot of hand work in the manufacture. Circa 1910.

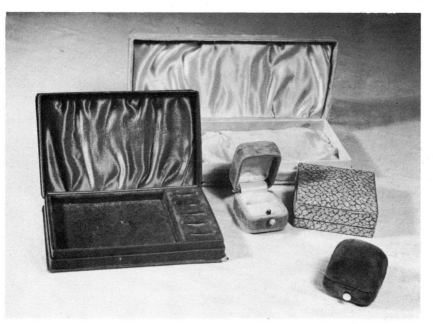

Box with slot in lid and lock is handmade and is probably a ballot box.

houses and human figures. All of these designs became stylized as they were adapted to the stencil method of decoration. The colors used in decorating eary tinware were soft and mu ed when made in New England. Tinware made in Pennsylvania was decorated with brighter colors and the motifs were similar to those used in decorating wooden boxes.

The earliest tinware was made with lap-over rather than welded seams and will show other evidence of having been made by hand. Since factories made tinware well into the nineteenth century in large quantities, it is really only the handmade and hand-decorated boxes that are of real value. These are the wares of the tinsmiths who hand-crafted each box. Spice boxes, trinket boxes, and document boxes are eagerly sought, and when the paint and decoration are in fairly good condition they are considered valuable examples of American folk art.

Chapter 13

BOXES OF POTTERY
AND PORCELAIN

WHILE one might search in vain through books written on the subjects of pottery or porcelain for illustrations of boxes made in those materials, the ceramics collector is aware that there have been many boxes made in pottery and porcelain that are representative of some of the finest ceramics in the world. Many of these boxes are excellent examples of the potter's art, with perfectly fitting covers and superb decoration. Ceramics have been used for boxes in two ways, both as the body of the boxes and as applied decoration, for many years.

The specialist pottery or porcelain collector, if he searches long and hard enough, will eventually find a box in no matter what area of ceramics he collects. For instance, a collector of Chinese porcelain should be aware that a great many boxes were made and while they are certainly not as plentiful today as plates or other ceramic shapes, it is not impossible to find one.

Porcelain boxes were made by Meissen manufacturers as well as Sèvres, Bow, Chelsea, and other European manufacturers of porcelain and china. Besides these early makers of porcelain, there are hundreds of examples of nineteenth-century art styles that are represented in ceramic boxes. These later examples are more readily available and sometimes less expensive.

As mentioned before, there are two basic ways in which pottery or porcelain were used in the design and manufacture of boxes. The first is the use of the ceramic material for the making of the box

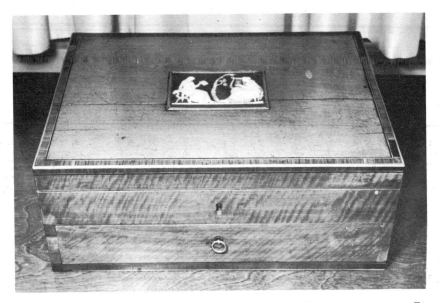

Sewing compendium of satinwood with Wedgwood plaque set in cover. Fittings are of carved ivory and cut steel. Secret drawer in side of box. Late eighteenth century.

Porcelain powder box, Meissen, decorated with flowers in high relief. Bronze doré mounts. Late eighteenth century.

(Above left) *Austrian jewel chest with hand-painted applied porcelain plaques. Each plaque is painted with a different scene. Gilded bronze mounts and hardware.* (Right) *View showing plaques. View showing interior of chest.*

itself, and the second is the application of medallions or panels set onto a box made of another material such as wood, ivory, metal, etc. This practice was particularly prevalent in the late eighteenth century, when Wedgwood made many cameos and medallions with classic subjects which were used by boxmakers as decoration.

Because the subject of pottery and porcelain boxes is as involved as the entire history of the art of ceramics since it began, we will limit ourselves here to discussion of two types of boxes that are available to a degree that collectors can find enough good examples of either. Both types can be purchased without too large an investment and both will increase in value as collections. One must assume that any collector making a large investment in a box made of pottery or porcelain will be armed with enough special knowledge so that he knows what he is purchasing.

The first ceramic boxes we will discuss will be those made by Wedgwood in England. Since this company has been in business for over two hundred years and has always produced a large quantity of boxes and plaques and medallions used as applied decoration for boxes, this would be an interesting category in which the collector could limit himself and still gather together boxes made in any decorative style of the past two centuries from neoclassic to modern. One might also further specialize in one of the many clay bodies used

Jewel chest with brass straps and Wedgwood cameo on lid. Circa 1850.

Brass collar box with Wedg-wood plaque inserted on lid.

by Wedgwood or in one particular color of pottery.

Perhaps the earliest boxes produced in which the Wedgwood enthusiast will have interest are those made out of wood, with applied Wedgwood medallions, by joiners and cabinetmakers in the eighteenth century. Wedgwood medallions were used for box decoration toward the end of the eighteenth century and often during the nineteenth century. To complicate matters further, there were many potters who copied Wedgwood's medallions. Also, not only British, but French, American, and German boxmakers used these medallions on their products so that applied Wedgwood can be found on boxes that were not made in England. Although Wedgwood marked all of his wares, there will be no visible mark on *applied* Wedgwood medallions because the mark is on the back. Therefore, the collector must have a great deal of knowledge of the subject matter used for these medallions by Wedgwood, the general appearance of early Wedgwood jasper ware, and other criteria before he can state for certain that a box with applied cameos or medallions is indeed Wedgwood. While the Wedgwood collector will care a great deal about authenticity, the box collector won't. It will make little difference to him who made the adornment for his box as long as he thinks it an unusual and attractive box. In any case, there is hardly an abundance of eighteenth-century applied Wedgwood boxes.

A type of box made by Wedgwood that is more apt to be collected today is the small jasper ware box. Those that are particularly de-

105

Small collection of Wedgwood jasper ware boxes. Lilac, green and blue with white applied decoration. If purchased new in unusual colors, these boxes soon become collector's items.

sirable are the boxes in unusual colors and combinations of colors. Wedgwood has made many colors of jasper ware besides the blue and white for which they are most noted. For instance, a collection of small jasper ware boxes might include a box with yellow ground and white relief, a box with a crimson ground, and one with the bright-blue ground that was made at the beginning of this century but is no longer being produced. While the red and yellow jasper ware is rare, today, it is not very old, and if purchased forty years ago when new it would have increased enormously in value. Unusual colors in jasper ware boxes are still being made. Lilac and salmon-pink are two colors that have been produced recently in limited amounts and then discontinued. A great many small boxes were made in both colors.

Obviously, the most valuable Wedgwood box collection would include only eighteenth- and early nineteenth-century patch boxes, etui, compendiums, snuffboxes, or tea caddies that are set with authentic Wedgwood medallions. These are, of course, in great demand by specialist Wedgwood collectors and are quite rare. However, the box collector should not overlook the possibilities of building excellent, increasingly valuable collections from new production. The subject of Wedgwood boxes is so vast that it can only be touched on here, and a great deal of further reading will be necessary for the neophyte to become aware of the many kinds of boxes available in this area of specialized collecting.

A second example of collectible ceramics box is Parian ware. Parian, a white porcelain made to imitate Italian marble, was produced in the last half of the nineteenth century in England and America. While Parian was developed mainly for statuary, a great many small boxes, enchantingly decorated, were also manufactured. These small white trinket boxes are sometimes embellished with the addition of color. Blue, brown, green, or pink slip often embellished the sides or tops of the boxes, somewhat in the manner of Wedgwood jasper ware. The designs and shapes of these boxes, however, are purely Victorian in appearance.

Bone china cigarette box. Blue luster with gold printed decoration. Iridescent mother-of-pearl glaze on interior. This "Dragon ware" made by Wedgwood at the beginning of this century is highly prized as a collectible item today. Boxes are rare.

(Below) Small collection of Parian boxes. Box on left has blue slip decoration.

Ceramic box with pale grey glaze, hand decorated with violets and gold insect. Marked: E. Gallé, Nancy. Gallé's pottery is not as well known as his art glass.

Enameled porcelain trinket box with brass trim.

(Below) "Rose tapestry" pattern of this box is in great demand by collectors. Marked: Royal Bayreuth, Bavaria.

There seems to be an almost endless variety of shapes and motifs used in the high relief decoration of Parian boxes. Birds' nests (with or without eggs), lions, lambs, sleeping babies, doves, and dogs are but a few of the motifs to be found adorning the covers of Parian ware. Most of the British-made boxes are marked by the companies that made them. Copeland, Minton, Mayer, and Meigh are a few of the companies to have manufactured this ware. The major American production of Parian was carried on in Bennington, Vermont.

There is a strong similarity between the motifs of the English- and American-made Parian so that one must assume that much of the Bennington ware was copied directly from British products. It is difficult to distinguish between them when they are unmarked. Devotees of Parian have little reverence for the small boxes and search for the statuary that was made earlier of a superior type of Parian. Therefore, there are still a great many Parian trinket boxes to be found by box collectors.

The above are just two suggestions for specialized collections of porcelain or pottery boxes. There are, of course, many other types of boxes to be found. Miniature bone-china boxes made by every important manufacturer in England, in all the popular patterns, can be collected. French and German porcelain boxes and Spanish and Italian pottery boxes can also be found. The possibilities are almost limitless in this field of collecting and the accumulation of such a collection can satisfy the lover of old or new china and pottery as well as the box enthusiast.

Chapter 14

BOXES DECORATED
AT HOME BY HAND

Some of the most charming old boxes that have come down to us were made and/or decorated by amateurs as a means of passing the time while keeping busy. Boxes have long been manufactured and left unfinished for the home decorator to decorate or embellish in some way. The decoration of boxes with needlework, dècoupage, paper filigree, beadwork, stenciling, and other forms of adornment has occupied the leisure time of many women since the seventeenth century. The popularity of all sorts of handwork becomes faddish among women, and many old styles of box decoration have been revived from time to time. Currently, it is "fashionable" to decorate boxes using the techniques and patterns of eighteenth-century French dècoupage. It is not unlikely that many of these boxes being decorated today with cut-out paper designs will be collector's items of the future.

Perhaps one of the most unique kinds of home-decorated box that has come down to us is the stump-work casket, the earliest of which were made in England around the middle of the seventeenth century. Panels of embroidery, worked by young girls, were mounted on boxes made by joiners expressly for that purpose. The fabric used was a heavy white satin and the work was done in a Jacobean, folk-embroidery, style of a pictorial nature. A three-dimensional technique which combined appliqué as well as every known kind of embroidery stitch was employed to depict a story from the Bible or other allegorical or historical theme. The materials used in stump

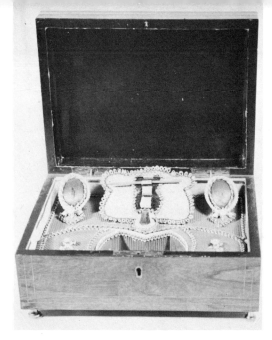

Sewing-music box was embellished by botany enthusiast with dried specimen of white lily. Interior of box shows fittings for sewing equipment. Music box is in bottom. Circa 1880.

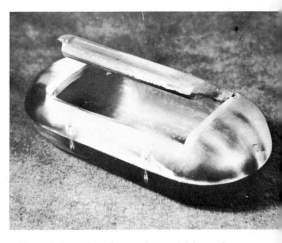

(Above) *Handmade snuff box of horn has perfectly fitting lid. American, Eighteenth century.*

(Left) *Old paper covered box was decorated with fashion plate from early magazine.*

Decoupage is still a popular craft for ladies. Card box and trinket box are modern using told techniques.

work were silk floss, silver and gold spangles, and bits and pieces of braid, lace, and ribbon. Beads were often used to embellish the panels, as were the eyes of peacock tail-feathers and human hair. The figures were often stuffed and then applied to give a three-dimensional effect.

Enough of these early stump-work caskets can be seen in museums of decorative arts to lead one to assume that this form of busywork for girls was rather popular. This style of embroidery was revived in England in the nineteenth century when there was a great revival of all types of needlework for ladies.

Another type of box decoration that was done at home in the seventeenth century in England was paper filigree work. This work was patterned after metal filigree and imitated the intricate scrollings and patterns seen in the gold and silver surfaces of boxes made of these more precious materials.

As in stump work, the boxes were made by joiners expressly for the purpose of being decorated with this rolled-paper technique. The material used in the decoration was vellum, parchment, or paper. Briefly, narrow strips of the paper were cut and rolled into tight cylinders. These were then glued to the surfaces of the box in various designs. When left unpainted, filigree boxes closely resembled intricately carved ivory. Many were painted silver or gold. Center medallions of colored flowers or garlands made from paper scrolls were also used as embellishments.

Toward the end of the eighteenth century, paper filigree work was revived with contemporary magazines providing printed patterns and instructions to follow. Special paper was also issued at this time for decorating the tea caddies, octagonal boxes, and jewel chests made with recessed panels especially for filigree work.

Beadwork has been another method of box decoration for the needleworker. Many beadwork boxes were made in Europe since the seventeenth century. A particularly charming type was made in England of small colored glass beads sewn to linen canvas panels which were then applied to wooden boxes. Some of these boxes have groups of flowers inside the lids that are wired and freestanding and resemble gardens. Few of these boxes survive outside of museums today, but since beadwork is once again fashionable, those who have become bored making bead flower arrangements might consider this more ambitious type of project.

When the above types of handwork were revived in the nineteenth century, Victorian motifs and styles prevailed. The techniques, however, were basically the same. A kind of box decoration

(Left) The making of small boxes has occupied many amateur woodworkers for centuries. This miniature desk, really a jewelry box, was made in Rhode Island at end of last century. (Right) This old snuff box was decorated with an Indian arrow head on lid.

Homemade jewel chest of Vermont marble slabs screwed into wood carcass. Edges are covered in red plush fabric. Circa 1900.

Glove box, dated February 22, 1908. These boxes were sold unfinished with stamped designs to be decorated at home by painting, wood-burning or carving.

that has prevailed and has enjoyed many periods of renewed popularity is *dècoupage* work. In recent years in America this craft has developed a large following, and classes and exhibits are given frequently. Reproductions of French printed papers have been made so that copies of earlier *dècoupage* can be made. When care is given to the choice of pattern and coloring and the cutting is intricately and carefully done, these boxes can be most charming.

Boxes have been made in the past that were covered with panels of needlepoint, crewel embroidery, inlaid shells, dried, pressed flowers, and many other types of fabric and materials. There were boxes made by the Flemish Art Company in America at the turn of the century that were stamped with *art nouveau* style floral designs meant for the wood-burning enthusiasts of the time. Some of the amateur decorators carved and painted as well as burnished these stamped patterns.

The above are but a few examples of boxes that were decorated at home and cherished by those whose busy hands made them. It is interesting that these "busywork" boxes were often made for one purpose . . . to contain the impedimenta of other types of busywork.

Chapter 15

CARE AND REPAIR
OF OLD BOXES

Often a collector of old boxes, upon finding an unusual box that he would like to add to his collection, will be faced with a dilemma. The price might be right, the box might be just what he has been hoping someday to find, but the condition will leave a lot to be desired. Sometimes, if the condition seems to be beyond repair, the box will be better left at the dealer's. However, there are many kinds of boxes that can be restored at home by the owner, who will derive more than a little satisfaction from having saved a desirable old box from the trash heap. Some defects are easily repairable while others are not.

One of the reasons for explaining in detail the kind of decoration and manner of materials from which papier-mâché and Japanese lacquer boxes were made was to give collectors some clue as to how these boxes should be treated when being cleaned or restored. Many papier-mâché boxes have lost much of their decoration from over-zealous maintenance in the past. In the case of decorated lacquer finishes, often too much care of the wrong kind is worse than total neglect.

The most effective and least harmful way to clean decorated papier-mâché boxes is to use a cream furniture polish very sparingly on a soft cloth and to rub gently. The polish should be wiped immediately with another dry, soft cloth. Goddard Furniture Cream will remove a hundred years of grime in a few minutes and restore the original luster to papier-mâché without seeming to harm painted,

116

Boxes incorporating several different materials require careful cleaning. Hand-painted bone china box (Wedgwood) is set in Sheffield silver base and has silver cover with ivory finial. Circa 1890.

(Right) Nineteenth century English brass lunch pail becomes attractive room accessory when carefully polished.

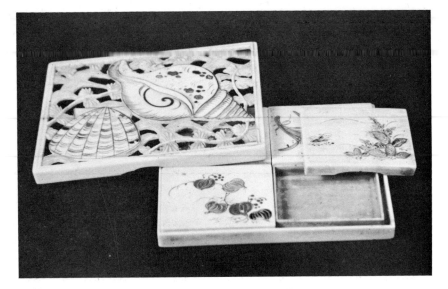

Four miniature boxes in a box. Carved and pierced ivory.

printed, or inlay decoration in any way. Any other good quality furniture cream should be as effective. For particularly grimy areas a soft cloth soaked in soapy warm water (not detergent) and wrung almost dry will work well. Dry any cleaned areas immediately with a soft cloth.

Beware of applying pressure to any areas that are hand painted. These areas should be treated very gently and if it is not absolutely necessary to clean a section of a box that is hand painted, don't. Never touch up the painted areas with oil paint or in any way attempt to restore a painted scene. This work is better left to professional restorers, or if the value of the box doesn't warrant the expense, leave the painting alone entirely. Some of the miniature paintings on the lids of papier-mâché boxes were done by very skilled and talented artists and are more valuable left in their original condition than they are if "restored" by an amateur.

The damage most commonly found in hinged-lid papier-mâché boxes such as tea caddies, jewel caskets, or writing boxes is that through long use and probably some abuse the hinges have pulled away from the box. This damage can be repaired with the use of plastic wood. Fill the area where the hinge has pulled away with the plastic wood and press the hinge into it while the lid is in a closed position. Bind the box tightly with string or tape using soft paper at the corners to prevent the lacquer from chipping. When the plastic wood is completely dried, pound cut-off straight pins or very small brass nails into the holes in the hinge where the original nails were. This should hold the hinges adequately. If the plastic wood is visible around the hinges it can be touched up with black India ink applied with a soft paint brush.

Often there are small chips at points of wear in the lacquer. These can also be touched up with India ink. Be very careful not to apply any pressure from the brush when doing this because the lacquer has a tendency to flake off further when wet. If mother-of-pearl inlay becomes loosened and falls out it can be glued back somewhat successfully with white plastic glue. Use the glue sparingly and wipe off any excess immediately. Gold lines that have worn away can be repainted. Use artists' gold powder for this purpose and apply with a very fine camel's-hair brush.

When polishing any brass or pewter trim or hardware on papier-mâché, the metal polish should be used with great care. Most of it is quite abrasive and will permanently dull the lacquer finish if any of it is allowed to remain very long. If any polish does get on the lacquer, wipe the area immediately with a soft cloth and a small amount of cream furniture wax and polish with a clean, soft, dry cloth.

Very little can be done to restore Japanese lacquer boxes that are not in good condition. Since good quality Japanese lacquer is so hard and impervious to damage from dampness and will take a lot of abuse, the really worthwhile pieces are usually in good condition when found. The boxes that are chipped or damaged are often of an inferior quality. Japanese lacquer boxes can be cleaned with cream

Two tortoise shell card cases and a carved tortoise shell snuff box. This is another material that requires careful handling and cleaning.

furniture wax in the same manner as described for papier-mâché above except that they will abide a more vigorous polishing.

Often an old box in extremely bad repair can be purchased for next to nothing at junk shops or auctions. The box collector would be wise to invest what little money is necessary to own a few of these, for often the parts, such as the hinges, brass strips, or nails, can be used in fixing other boxes that are in repairable condition.

Cream furniture polish or paste wax on a damp cloth and vigorous polishing will restore the patina on neglected wood boxes. In restoring most old wood boxes this treatment is all that is needed. A few scratches or dents do not detract much from old wood and unless there are really bad damages it is better for the amateur to leave them alone. Veneered-wood boxes present somewhat more of a problem when they are in need of repair. Since it is difficult to match wood grains or to recut and reglue loosened veneer, if a box has artistic or monetary value it should be repaired by an experienced furniture restorer. Veneered boxes should be polished along, rather than against, the grain. Water should never be used for cleaning purposes as it will loosen the fish glue that adheres the veneer to the carcass of the box. Again, use caution when polishing brass

Filagree silver box of Eastern origin would lose patina if too vigorously polished.

Enameled silver box with center painting and lapis lazuli panels on lid requires careful cleaning to avoid damaging enamel. Swiss, 1875.

or other metal hardware or decoration so that no metal polish is allowed to remain on the wood.

Sometimes the interior of a box will show more wear than the exterior and will require some restoration. This can easily be done by relining (or lining) the box with fabric or paper. The ideal kind of lining would be a material of the same period as the box itself, but old fabrics are not easily found today. There are fabric companies that specialize in damasks, velvets, and silk materials that are reproductions of eighteenth-century fabrics. Scraps or samples of this kind of material can sometimes be obtained from decorators or upholsterers, who are often happy to get rid of them. Samples of reproduction wallpapers are not difficult to obtain, either.

In order to make a lining for a box, cut panels to fit the sides, bottom, and inside of cover from a sheet of thin cardboard. Cut these panels slightly smaller than you want the finished panels to be. How much smaller these panels are cut will depend upon the type of fabric or paper you are planning to use. Obviously, a heavy damask or velvet will require the cardboard to be cut a little smaller than a thinner fabric or paper. Lay the cardboard panels on the fabric or lining paper and cut around them leaving a half-inch of lining material on all sides.

121

Working with one panel at a time, cover one side of the cardboard with a thin coat of white glue and press the fabric or paper to it, stretching the fabric so that there are no wrinkles. Turn the cardboard over so that the fabric side is down and slit the four corners of the fabric with small, sharp scissors so that they will overlap. Apply glue to one-half inch from edge on all four sides of the cardboard, working with one side at a time. Glue the excess fabric to the cardboard, pulling gently so that there are no wrinkles. When heavy material is used you may have to trim some of the fabric at the corners so that they are not dog-eared. When all four sides are glued, place a couple of heavy books on top of them until the glue is completely dry.

Cover all six panels in the above fashion. When they are all prepared they can be glued into the sides, top, and bottom of the box. It is possible to glue some fabrics or papers directly into the box without using the cardboard, particularly if the fabric is heavy enough so that the glue will not come through to spot it. However, the first method is by far the more desirable for a finished appearance.

The lead-paper-lined compartments of tea caddies can be restored if the old paper is torn or in poor condition. First, scrape all the old paper from the box and replace it by gluing aluminum kitchen foil, dull side out, to the sides and bottom. Measure and cut each panel one-half inch larger on all sides. Carefully fold each side one-half inch toward the center so that the folded edges are straight. This gives more strength and a better-looking finish. It is also easier to obtain straight edges when the foil edges are folded rather than cut. Glue these panels into the box one at a time, pressing the foil as you work so that it conforms to the shape of the compartment. While the glue is drying, press several times again. Foil wallpaper may also be used for lining tea caddies.

You will find that your bottle of white glue (Borden's Elmer's Glue-All is an excellent brand) is indispensable for all sorts of minor repairs on boxes made of a variety of materials. Inlay of ivory, mother-of-pearl, wood, or bone can be reglued if it has come loose. Using a single-edge, new razor blade, scrape off all excess glue from the loose piece of inlay and scrape as much glue as possible from the depression where the inlay loosened. Blow away all loose dry glue and wipe out with a dry cloth. Apply glue to the piece of inlay. Press it into its proper place and wipe away any wet glue that might squeeze up along the edge. If possible—that is, if the inlay is from a

This silver cigarette case, enameled in bright colors should be polished with care, also. Swedish, circa 1880.

flat surface—place a heavy weight on top until the glue has dried.

Because boxes ordinarily do not get the same kind of wear and abuse as do many other types of collectible items, they can usually be found in fairly decent condition regardless of the material from which they were made. The type of restoration most often needed is usually a good thorough cleaning. Since every possible material has been used in boxmaking and often a single box can incorporate several materials, it is necessary to know the proper preparations to use for the various materials most often found in old boxes.

First, don't attempt to clean ivory with anything but a mild detergent-and-water solution. Use cotton balls for this and wring them out as much as is practical before using. Dry right away with clean cotton. If the ivory has yellowed, leave it alone. Aside from washing, there isn't much you can do. Use the above method for cleaning mother-of-pearl, also. Tortoise-shell should be cleaned similarly except that a mild soap should be used rather than a detergent.

Ormolu may be cleaned with a weak solution of an ammonia-based cleaner (Soilax) and water. Use one teaspoonful to a cup of warm water. Be extremely careful not to get any of this solution on the rest of the box. It could easily ruin a wood finish. Brass and copper can be cleaned with any good commercial preparation made for either of these metals. Decide before you begin to rub how "new" you want your box to look. On many old boxes a "good as new" appearance may be somewhat disappointing. It takes many years for metal to acquire a patina which is often more attractive than new-looking metal. Enameled metal boxes can be cleaned with mild soap and water if cotton is used in the application and the box is dried immediately. If there is any indication of the enamel lifting or if there are any cracks or dents, don't attempt to clean it.

In the case of wood boxes such as veneered knife cases or compendiums, remember that part of the value of an antique is in the patina and finish. Unless the condition of the finish is so poor that it is unsightly, make no attempt to have this type of box refinished. A good rubbing with paste wax will remove most dirt and restore the old wood. There's no reason why something a hundred years old or more should look as though it were made yesterday.

Decorative boxes of this type are easily found at flea markets and second hand stores. It is made of papier-mâché and was used as gift box for made in Japan items at turn of the century. Yellow with hand-painted flowers.

Chapter 16

WHERE TO LOOK FOR COLLECTIBLE BOXES

GIVEN a much wider variety than most collectors of antiques enjoy, those of us who are enamored of boxes can search for them almost anywhere that old things are sold. With the exception of miniature boxes made from precious or semiprecious materials, boxes have long been the orphans of the antiques trade. There have always been so many of them around, and they do not readily fit into the many categories in which antique dealers are apt to specialize. With the exception, again, of the miniatures, there has been little literature written about boxes as a category for collecting. This, of course, is fortunate for the collector because books about a particular kind of antique tend to raise the value and create a market for hitherto unheralded collectibles.

There are many ways of putting together a box collection. The first, and from a value standpoint, the most desirable, is to collect one kind or category of boxes. For instance, a collection of tea caddies, particularly the fruit-shaped wood variety, becomes more valuable as a collection than would each individual caddy considered separately. The decorative and historical value of a collection of one kind of box will grow as the collection grows.

Obviously, where the collector searches for additions to his collection will depend upon the kind of box he collects and the relative scarcity of his category of collecting. One would not expect to find a Battersea or Staffordshire enamel box in a junk shop, whereas the possibility of coming across a fine example of Japanese lacquer in

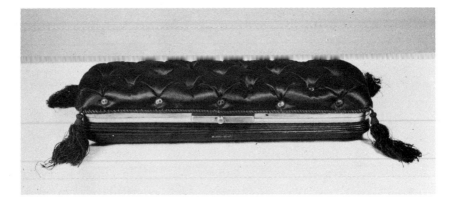

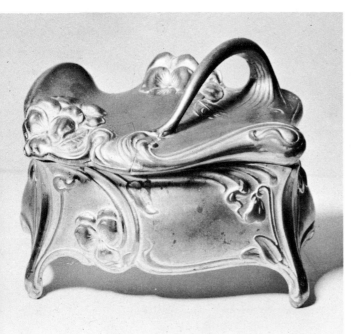

(Above) *Victorian jewel case covered in royal purple satin with brass frame. Accordion-pleated leather side panels make case expandable.*

(Left) *Bronzed white metal jewel casket is typical of the mass produced articles in high art nouveau style made in the early part of this century. Now sought by collectors of that period, these caskets were easily found at flea markets only a few years ago.*

the same store will lead the veteran collector to search in every second-hand dealer's store that he passes.

For boxes of obvious value, the collector will do well to find a dealer who specializes in his particular category, to establish a friendly relationship with that dealer, and to trust his judgment as to authenticity. Since most boxes, whether made by first-rate craftsmen or decorated by important artists, are not signed or otherwise

126

identifiable, only an expert's opinion will verify the age and value of an item. An honest dealer will tell the collector how much, if any, restoration has been done and will verify the age of manufacture to the best of his ability. Reliable antique dealers are to be found in every major city of the world. It is up to the collector to decide just how reliable a particular dealer is.

An easy method for finding antique dealers and studying the kind of wares they sell is to attend the antique shows and fairs in the larger cities to which the dealers bring representative examples of their stock. Boxes are always displayed and sold in abundance at these shows, for a very good reason. They are easy to pack and most are not as breakable in shipment as other types of antiques. At the larger antique shows the collector can find almost anything in which he might be interested, from primitive wood kitchen-storage boxes to Russian enamel. The dealers who specialize, for instance, in Wedgwood pottery or Chinese export porcelain will have boxes made of their particular specialty among their other wares. When these dealers are gathered together at an antiques show, it is a simple matter for the collector to compare prices for similar boxes

(Below) *Crystal box with brass cover. Cover is enameled in iridescent blue.*

(Right) *Desk box, oak. Movable calendar tells day of week as well as date. Has lift top and one drawer. Tambour front pulls down over file and locks. Circa 1900.*

owned by the various dealers and to study their condition, also.

Since some of the dealers who participate in antique shows do not have shops, but sell only at a few shows a year which they attend, there is always a possibility of finding a "sleeper" or something that the dealer owns, but does not realize the value of. Armed with some specialized knowledge and the collector's passion for finding and owning that which he collects, the possibility of spotting an interesting collectible box always prevails at antique shows.

Another good source for searching for boxes is the auction house. There are many types of auctions and auctioneers and those which the collector patronizes will depend upon what he collects and how much time and money he is willing to spend in the pursuit. The leading auction houses will, of course, carry the most desirable merchandise. Catalogues of the items to be auctioned are available in advance, and descriptions, usually accurate, are given of each item, so that the collector can decide ahead of time what he would like to bid on and how high he is willing to go in order to add to his collection the item to be auctioned. These catalogues also contain information for the collector that is of value in learning about antiques. Occasionally, an entire collection will be auctioned that will give the new collector some idea of what is available in his category and what the going prices are. Price lists are also available after an auction.

(Left) Blue glass cosmetic box with hand-painted medallion on lid. Embossed and gilded. (Right) Opaline glass box with brass frame. Boxes similar to this are still being made in Italy.

(Left) *Eighteenth century cut crystal box with silver gilt frame. This box would be a "find" for any collector.* (Right) *Amber glass casket with bronze mounts. White and grey enamel motifs. Circa 1890.*

These auctions, on the whole, set the prices of many collectible items.

It is not advisable for the neophyte collector, no matter how affluent, to plunge headlong into bidding on valuable items at one of these auctions. Once he has studied the catalogue and, preferably, the merchandise to be auctioned, he might consider asking a dealer to bid for him. Most antique dealers will do this for a small commission and their presence and advice may be well worth the investment. Specialist dealers often will extend each other the courtesy of not bidding against each other at an auction, whereas this courtesy certainly does not prevail where a collector is concerned. Dealers have attempted to band together in order to control, to some extent, the prices at auction of the items in which they specialize. With the scarcity of antiques and the growth in the number of collectors, an adequate supply of stock has become a major problem for the dealers, and auctions are, for them, a major source for restocking their dwindling supplies of desirable items. Therefore, it is always best to have at least one dealer on your side, especially if the item you hope to own is particularly old and desirable from the collector's standpoint. A favorite dealer may be loath to forego the eighteenth-century tea caddy for a small commission when he could visualize a larger profit if he purchased it for his shop, but he is willing to do

Yellow cameo glass box with deep blue overlay. Brass cover is heavily jeweled.

Art nouveau glass box. Opaline with decoration of prange tiger lilies and green foliage. Signed: Daume, Nancy. Boxes of this type are more rare than the art vases made by the same company.

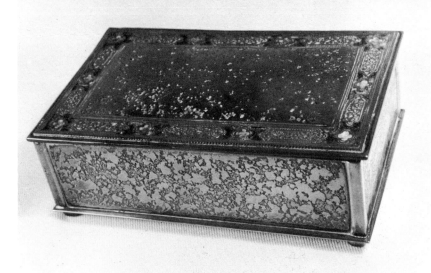

Cigarette box. Brass with copper lid enameled in shades of iridescent purple. Marked: Louis C. Tiffany Furnaces, Favrille, 130. Tiffany boxes such as these suffered a period of unpopularity when they could be purchased for very little. This is no longer true.

this favor for a collector who is also a client. He hopes to find an item that he can sell to the collector another time, on which he can make his usual profit.

Another type of auction that is sometimes a fertile source for nineteenth-century boxes is the smaller estate auction. These are auctions held in smaller cities and towns and the quality of merchandise will vary from very high to very poor. The auctioneers will vary accordingly, also. Many are very honest while others require that the bidder be armed with a lot of knowledge and much less eagerness for acquisition than most collectors have. At this type of auction there might be little or no opportunity for those in attendance to inspect the items to be auctioned. In this case, the collector is at the mercy of the auctioneer to learn of the condition of the box (or any other item) to be auctioned. A great many fakes and reproductions are passed off as old in this manner and the buyer must, at all times, beware. It is not unusual for an auctioneer to fatten even a bona fide estate auction with other, less desirable, items of more than questionable value.

When the collector can trust his own judgment both as to artistic and monetary value, he can safely attend auctions and often find very desirable items without being carried away by the fever that attacks many auction goers. One will have to be his own judge of whether it is worth it to sit through the bidding on worn-out linens and dented pots for the possibility of obtaining that papier-mâché glove box for half of what one might be asked by a dealer. Many country auctions are more informative for those interested in crowd psychology than they are for those interested in antiques.

Flea markets, street fairs, or any other place where second-hand household items are sold may be a source for the box collector. Tag sales held in houses are another source. Good old Victorian boxes are found in attics and cellars, where they are often put to use as containers for nails or other small items. Obviously, there is little chance of finding an old silver snuffbox serving this purpose, but it wouldn't be unusual for an old Shaker box or even a Victorian papier-mâché jewel box to be serving this useful but destructive function.

Small collection of silver boxes is attractive on a table. All boxes are of Englis' make except the snuff box, center left, which is French. Box at top left is ·vood inlaid with silver.

Chapter 17

HOW TO USE OLD BOXES
DECORATIVELY IN YOUR HOME

W HILE the foregoing chapters place emphasis on some of the various types of boxes that might be of interest to collectors, the chances are that most collectors will be apt to purchase any kind of old boxes that appeal to them and will use most of the smaller boxes as decorative accessories in their homes. The appeal of old wood, lacquer work, pottery, or brass is more easily and usually less expensively expressed in the purchase and ownership of boxes than in larger pieces of antique furniture.

When considering display space, obviously a collection of miniature boxes such as snuffboxes or vinaigrettes presents less of a problem than the same amount of tea caddies or writing boxes. However, these larger boxes are attractive and gain importance as a collection when arranged together on shelves on a living-room or dining-room wall.

It is the larger boxes, the plain mahogany boxes with brass hardware, that were never thought important enough to be of interest to collectors that have now come into their own. These boxes can serve a very important function in today's style of eclectic and period decoration. Small end tables have always been the most difficult type of antique furniture for decorators to find. Therefore, one searches for substitutes to serve the same function as an end table that will be in keeping with other antiques in a room. This is where the old boxes made of wood with simple lines and having only the old brasses as decoration (compendiums, writing boxes, small chests,

(Left) *Embossing, piercing and engraving are only a few of the methods used to decorate silver. This group is attractive display.*

(Below left) *Early nineteenth century writing box can become attractive and useful foyer table when placed on specially built stand.*

(Below) *Small campaign chest with brass mounts gains decorative importance when placed on specially designed stand.*

(Left) *Two small chests of Oriental design become useful and decorative tables in small library.* (Right) *Second view of same chests.*

and caskets) have begun to serve an entirely different purpose from that for which they were originally made.

Many of the Victorian jewel chests and compendiums are large enough to be used as end tables without the addition of a stand. Some of the smaller boxes can be given stands which are specially built to hold them. As long as the stands are in scale with the boxes for which they were made and are made of a wood that can be stained the approximate color of the box, this is an excellent method of solving the problem of providing a table on which to place an ash tray or a glass.

Any cabinetmaker should be proficient enough to make the type of stand that would be suitable for holding an old box. Square, tapered legs are usually in keeping with the plain eighteenth-century boxes. The talented craftsman can attempt a stand with bamboo-turned legs which are graceful for this purpose. The stands are made so that the box rests on an inner lip and can be removed. This way no dam-

135

Nineteenth century copy of earlier jewel chest is large enough to become table in contemporary setting.

Chest is made of marquetry inlay and is attractive opened or closed.

age is done to the box and no screws or nails are needed to hold it in place.

Brass-trimmed camphorwood captain's chests and other large chests are a solution to the lack of the functional coffee table. Since this type of low table is an innovation of designers and decorators

136

Chinese lacquered jewel chest with mother-of-pearl inlay, brass trimmed wood desk box and tea caddy add decorative interest to library shelves.

of our century, there are no antique coffee tables to be had. The low chest is usually the proper height for use in front of a sofa and can be lacquered to make the surface water and alcohol proof. Lacquering also solves the problem of having to polish the brasses that were used on these chests. A seaman's chest, used in this manner, is placed with the front facing the center of the room and the back toward the sofa. These same chests can be used against a long wall and serve a double function as a table or bench for extra seating.

Many smaller chests and boxes can also serve as small tables to place in front of a sofa. These are particularly effective when they can be found in pairs and can be placed together so that the surfaces of both can be put to use. In an era where beautiful wood grains, carefully matched, are almost never found in new furniture, these small decorative chests and boxes are avidly sought by those who revere the artistry and craftsmanship of the old cabinetmakers and joiners.

Smaller old boxes can serve as decorative objects in almost any room in the house. Often, the studied placement of a collection of old boxes between the books on a library shelf can provide a decorative and interesting focal point in a room. They can also serve a double function as book ends.

The use of old boxes as containers for dried flower arrangements can be the subject of a book in itself. Opened hinged-lid boxes, es-

137

(Left) *Satinwood wine cooler, Circa 1800, can be adapted to modern decoration as attractive planter.* (Right) *Decorated lacquer jewel chest with ornate brasses and painted applied ivory figures can be used as small end table.*

pecially those lined with attractive paper or fabric, provide handsome containers for dried arrangements if the floral material is carefully chosen to coordinate with the container and the room in which the arrangement is to be placed. Scale and color will be important factors to consider when making a lasting arrangement of this type.

Old tin store boxes are attractive accessories in country-style kitchens and family rooms. Shaker boxes and other old functional wood boxes are just as practical and attractive as they were a hundred years ago.

Old boxes, no matter of what material or style of decoration, have a way of finding their own resting places in new settings. Many old boxes can still fulfill their original functions while others are adapted for new purposes their makers could never have foreseen. Unlike many other small decorative collectible items, boxes help relieve clutter rather than add to it. The incurable box collector already knows what the largest boxes can be used for. He keeps his small boxes in them.

138

BIBLIOGRAPHY

Andrews, Edward Deming and Faith. *Religion in Wood: A Book on Shaker Furniture*. Bloomington and London: Indiana University Press, 1966.
——— *Shaker Furniture: The Craftsmanship of an American Communal Sect*. New York: Dover Publications, Inc., 1950.
Aronson, Joseph. *The Encyclopedia of Furniture*. New York: Crown Publishers, Inc., 1965.
Backlin, Landman and Shapiro, Edna. *The Story of Porcelain*. New York: The Odyssey Press, Inc., 1965.
Bedford, John. *All Kinds of Small Boxes*. New York: Walker and Company, 1964.
——— *The Collecting Man*. New York: David McKay Company, Inc., 1968.
Bjerkoe, Ethel Hall. *Decorating For and With Antiques*. New York: Doubleday & Company, Inc., 1950.
Brackett, Oliver. *English Furniture Illustrated*. New York: The Macmillan Company, 1950.
Brinkley, F. *China: Its History, Arts and Literature*. Boston and Tokyo: J. B. Millet Company, 1902.
——— *Japan: Its History, Arts and Literature*. Boston and Tokyo: J. B. Millet Company, 1902.
Butler, Joseph T. *American Antiques, 1800–1900*. New York: The Odyssey Press, Inc., 1965.
Clifford, Chandler R. *Period Furnishings: An Encyclopedia of Historical Furniture, Decorations and Furnishings*. New York: Clifford and Lawton, 1914.
Cole, Ann Kilborn. *The Golden Guide to American Antiques*. New York: The Golden Press, Inc., 1967.
Constantino, Ruth. *How to Know French Antiques*. New York: New American Library, 1961.
Delieb, Eric. *Silver Boxes*. New York: Clarkson N. Potter, Inc., 1968.

Dreppard, Carl W. *First Reader for Antique Collectors.* Garden City: Doubleday & Company, Inc., 1954.

———— *The Primer of American Antiques.* Garden City: Doubleday & Company, Inc., 1944.

———— Guild, Lurelle Van Arsdale. *New Geography of American Antiques.* New York: Award Books, 1928.

Earle, Alice Morse. *China Collecting in America.* New York: Charles Scribner's Sons, 1892.

Eberlein, Harold D. and Ramsdell, Roger W. *The Practical Book of Chinaware.* Philadelphia and New York: J. B. Lippincott Company, 1925.

Fastnedge, Ralph. *English Furniture Styles: From 1500 to 1830.* Harmonsworth: Penguin Books, Ltd., 1955.

Fedderson, Martin. *Japanese Decorative Art.* New York: Thomas Yoseloff, 1962.

Godden, Geoffrey A. *An Illustrated Encyclopaedia of British Pottery and Porcelain.* New York: Crown Publishers, Inc., 1966.

———— *Encyclopaedia of British Pottery and Porcelain Marks.* New York: Crown Publishers, Inc., 1964.

Grotz, George. *The Furniture Doctor.* Garden City: Doubleday and Company, Inc., 1962.

Hartmann, Sadakichi. *Japanese Art.* Boston: L. C. Page & Company, 1904.

Hayward, Helena. *Eighteenth Century English Enamel. Part I; Battersea. Part II; The Staffordshire Factories. Part III; Birmingham, Liverpool and the Independent Decorators.* New York: Antiques. May, July, September 1952.

Hayward, Helena, Editor. *The Connoisseur's Handbook of Antique Collecting.* New York: Hawthorn Books, Inc., 1960.

Henderson, James. *Silver Collecting for Amateurs.* New York: Barnes and Noble, Inc., 1965.

Hinkley, F. L. *A Directory of Antique Furniture: The Authentic Classification of European and American Designs for Professionals and Connoisseurs.* New York: Crown Publishers, Inc., 1953.

Honey, W. B. *Wedgwood Ware.* London: Faber and Faber, 1948.

Hughes, G. Bernard. *Victorian Pottery and Porcelain.* New York: The Macmillan Company, 1959.

Hughes, Bernard and Therle. *Small Antique Furniture.* London: Lutterworth Press, 1958.

Hughes, Therle. *Small Antiques for the Collector.* New York: The Macmillan Company, 1964.

———— *Small Decorative Antiques.* London: Lutterworth Press, 1959.

Huth, Hans. *Russian Lacquer.* New York: Antiques, December 1967.

Kahle, Katherine Morrison. *An Outline of Period Furniture.* New York: G. P. Putnam's Sons, 1929.

Kettel, Russell H. *The Pine Furniture of Early New England*. New York: Dover Publications, Inc., 1929.

Kimerley, W. L. *How to Know Period Styles in Furniture*. Grand Rapids: Periodical Publishing Company, 1917.

Lancaster, Clay. *The Japanese Influence in America*. New York: Walton H. Rawls, 1963.

Lavine, Sigmund A. *Handmade in England: The Tradition.of British Craftsmen*. New York: Dodd, Mead & Company, Inc., 1968.

Lichten, Frances. *Decorative Art of Victoria's Era*. New York: Charles Scribner's Sons, 1950.

McBride, Robert Medill. *A Treasury of Antiques*. New York: Robert M. McBride & Company, 1939.

———— *Furnishing with Antiques*. New York: Robert M. McBride & Company, 1939.

McClinton, Katherine Morrison. *A Handbook of Popular Antiques*. New York: Bonanza Books, 1945.

———— *The Complete Book of American Country Antiques*. New York: Coward-McCann, Inc., 1967.

Mankowitz, Wolf. *Wedgwood*. London: Spring Books, 1953.

Martin, John Stuart, Editor. *A Picture History of Russia*. New York: Crown Publishers, Inc., 1945.

Miller, Edgar G., Jr. *American Antique Furniture: A Book for Amateurs*. Volumes I and II. Baltimore: The Lord Baltimore Press, 1937.

Mills, John F. *The Care of Antiques*. New York: Hastings House Publishers, Inc., 1964.

Ormsbee, Thomas H. *Care and Repair of Antiques*. New York: Gramercy Publishing Company, 1949.

———— *Early American Furniture Makers: A Social and Biographical Study*. New York: Tudor Publishing Company, 1930.

Parke-Bernet Galleries, Inc. Auction Catalogues: *Russian Objets d'Art*. November 8 and 9, 1963. *Japanese and Chinese Art*. February 1 and 2, 1963. *Valuable English XVIII Century Furniture and Decorations*. January 30 and 31, 1959. New York: Parke-Bernet Galleries, Inc.

Parsons, Frank A. *Interior Decorations: Its Principles and Practices*. New York: Doubleday, Page and Company, 1929.

Rheims, Maurice. *The Flowering of Art Nouveau*. New York: Harry N. Abrams, Inc., 1966.

Robacher, Carl F. *Pennsylvania Dutch Stuff: A Guide to Country Antiques*. Philadelphia: University of Pennsylvania Press, 1944.

Savage, George. *A Concise History of Interior Decoration*. New York: Grosset and Dunlap, Inc., 1966.

———— *The Antique Collector's Handbook*. London: Spring Books, 1959.

Schmutzler, Robert. *Art Nouveau*. New York: Harry N. Abrams, Inc., 1964.

Symonds, R. W., Whineray, B. B. *Victorian Furniture*. London: Country Life, Limited, 1962.

Toller, Jane. *Papier-Mâché in Great Britain and America*. Newton: Charles T. Branford Company, 1962.

Towne, Morgan. *Treasures in Truck and Trash*. Doubleday and Company, Inc., 1950.

Tunis, Edwin. *Colonial Craftsmen and the Beginnings of American Industry*. New York: The World Publishing Company, 1965.

Viaux, Jacqueline. *French Furniture*. New York: G. P. Putnam's Sons, 1964.

Ward, Bradley. *For Dippers and Sniffers Only!* Dublin, New Hampshire: *Yankee*, Yankee, Inc. February 1969.

Williamson, Scott Graham. *The American Craftsman*. New York: Crown Publishers, Inc., 1949.

Winchester, Alice. *How to Know American Antiques*. New York: New American Library, 1951.

142

INDEX